MODERN QUILTING

FROM FIRST STITCHES
TO FINISHING TOUCHES

MODERN QUILTING

FROM FIRST STITCHES TO FINISHING TOUCHES

Cait Moreton-Lisle

THE CROWOOD PRESS

CONTENTS

CHAPTER 1

INTRODUCTION

This book is for anyone who wants to make modern quilts or learn more about quilting. From demystifying the language of quilting with a comprehensive dictionary, to step-by-step guides walking you through all the stages of making a quilt alongside discussions of which materials and equipment are most helpful for each task, to block tables with all the formulae you need to design and create your own block-based quilts, *Modern Quilting* is a one-stop reference guide you'll want to keep by your side throughout your quilting journey.

Have you never touched a needle and thread? No problem! This book will give you the confidence you need to take your very first steps into the quilting world by building a solid foundation of core skills that will enable you to make not just your first quilt but everything beyond.

Do you have a few quilts under your belt but still feel like there's room to improve? Welcome! This book will support you in using and developing the skills you've already acquired while encouraging you to explore a variety of quilt patterns and helping you to develop your own unique style.

Are you an experienced quilter looking for a handy reference guide paired with some exciting modern quilt patterns? Come on in! Whether you've never quite built up the courage to attempt curves or Foundation Paper Piecing is your foe, this book will guide you through everything you feel you should know.

Constellations is an example of modern traditionalism using bright solid colours to update classic quilt blocks.

WHAT IS A MODERN QUILT?

To start, what makes a quilt a 'modern' quilt? At its most basic, a quilt is two layers of fabric separated by a thick layer of batting and sewn together, typically with a bound edge enclosing the layers. The Oxford Dictionary describes a quilt as 'a warm bed covering made of padding enclosed between layers of fabric and kept in place by lines of stitching, typically applied in a decorative design.' While this is of course one way of describing a quilt, a quilt is so much more than that. It's a warm hug. It's an expression of creativity. It's a piece of art. A quilt can be whatever its maker wants it to be. One thing quilters universally agree on, however, is that a quilt is decidedly *not* a blanket.

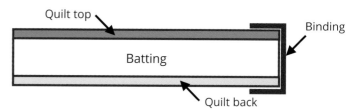

The term 'modern quilting' encompasses a huge range of quilting styles which have been inspired by modern design principles, colours and fabrics. There is no universally accepted definition but the Modern Quilt Guild (MQG), a global group dedicated to supporting and encouraging the growth and development of modern quilting, has a certain authority on the matter. Rather than giving a specific definition, the MQG gives a broad and non-definitive list of characteristics that they see as common in many modern quilts:

- Bold use of colour.
- High contrast and graphic areas of colour.
- Improvisational piecing.
- Minimalism.
- Maximalism.
- Expansive negative space.
- Alternate grid work (non-traditional arrangement of blocks – for example, not a 4×4 grid).
- Modern traditionalism (in which traditional quilt blocks and styles are reimagined using modern quilting elements, such as asymmetry, colour, and scale).

Flowers is an example of minimalism, with bold use of colour and negative space being employed to create a simple yet impactful design.

Orange Blossoms uses alternative grid work in combination with modern traditionalism to create a unique quilt.

No quilt is perfect and these misaligned points in Blue Days do not detract from the overall visual impact.

In contrast, the Festival of Quilts (Europe's largest quilting show) defines modern quilts more specifically as: '[Q]uilts that are minimalist with clean, modern design and a strong visual impact. They often use asymmetry, improvisational piecing, a reinterpretation of traditional blocks or the lack of a visible block structure. A feeling of space is often achieved [using] negative space. They are machine or hand quilted in a way that is sympathetic to the design.'

The differences and overlaps between these definitions show just how fluid and hard to define modern quilting is. At their core though, modern quilts reflect the styles and influences of the time: they are frequently bold, usually colourful and often use graphic design elements. To borrow a popular proverb, 'modern is in the eye of the quilter'.

THERE ARE NO QUILT POLICE

There are no quilt police so don't worry if your first, second or even hundredth tries at making a quilt aren't perfect. They are all perfectly imperfect and all that matters is that you enjoy making them. Not every point has to be exact for a quilt to be beautiful and not every stitch has to be faultless for it to be worthy of gifting to a loved one or taking pride of place on your wall.

Do not be afraid of flaws. Quilting is a creative hobby, and you are making something beautiful by hand – errors are natural and even the best quilters are quick to point out the mistakes in their work. Don't become your own quilt police by immediately pointing out the flaws when showing off your hard work – most people can't even see them! When viewing a piece of art, the best distance is often thought to be two to three times the diagonal length of the piece – if you can't see any mistakes clearly from that distance, the odds are no-one else can either. Remember that the little quirks are what makes something unique and precious, and your quilts are no exception.

MYTH BUSTING

There are lots of assumptions about quilting that can make it seem very intimidating. However, many of them are nothing more than stories in need of some myth busting:

It's too hard
Everything can seem hard when you first start out, but this book is here to walk you through every stage of making a quilt step by step. If you find it overwhelming, try not to focus on the big picture and instead focus on just the current step.

Quilting is old fashioned
Despite being rooted in centuries-old traditions, quilting is only as old fashioned as the fabrics and quilt patterns you choose to use.

I need to have a sewing room to be a quilter
Whether you're lucky enough to have a dedicated craft room or you can only carve out a corner of the dining table after putting the kids to bed, anywhere can be a quilting space.

I need to buy lots of expensive equipment to start
While you will need some gear to get started, it doesn't have to break the bank. Chapter 3 helps you pick out the absolute essentials alongside discussion of some of the many nice-to-have options available.

I have to make the quilt exactly as the pattern says I should
Quilt patterns should be viewed as recipes for you to tweak and adjust according to your personal taste. Change colours, switch solids for patterns, go scrappy, you should feel free to make it your own. It is your quilt after all.

I'm not a real quilter, I haven't even finished one quilt
It doesn't matter if you've just started, have been working on one quilt for years or have a pile of partly made projects: you're a quilter.

Quilts take too long to make
Yes, quilts can take a long time to make but if you choose a simple pattern and put aside a weekend or two, you can achieve a lot in a small amount of time. If you're really pushed for time, consider trying a quilted cushion.

I'm too slow
It doesn't matter how long it takes you: many quilters work on projects for years. Quilting is a slow craft and is about enjoying the process – some quilters have projects decades old that they still enjoy chipping away at now and again.

I'm doing it the wrong way
You don't have to follow the rules – if you want to do something a different way, go for it. Remember, there are no quilt police.

SUSTAINABLE SEWING

How to be sustainable while quilting is a growing area of concern for many as people become more environmentally minded and conscious of the impact their hobby has on the planet. While it's tempting to think that you're just one quilter and how big an impact can you have, when you look at the $4billion+ quilting industry it forms a huge part of the textile industry with widespread global impact including textile waste, water consumption and increased carbon emissions. This is not to say you shouldn't ever buy new fabric or indulge in the latest gadget, but there are small things you can do to incorporate more sustainable quilting practices with relative ease.

Using leftover scraps and fabrics from other projects is an excellent way to start incorporating sustainable practices into your quilting.

Please remember that the following are simply suggestions. Not everyone will be able to afford or access organic fabrics and while spray basting may not be great environmentally, it could be the best option for someone with arthritis or a limb difference. Making quilting more sustainable is a community effort and no-one should be made to feel bad if they don't (or can't) do everything suggested here.

Reduce

The easiest way to start incorporating sustainability into your quilting practice is with mindful consumption. Simply put, mindful consumption is about being more conscious of your choices as a consumer and making more informed purchasing decisions.

Shop your collection first

Most quilters quickly build up more fabric than they could use in years, yet many often choose to buy new for each project instead of using what they have. Try challenging yourself to only shop from your collection for your next project – you might be surprised at how easily you can do this.

Shop for specific projects

The temptation to buy a few cute fat quarters or a half yard of that must-have fabric whenever visiting your local quilt shop is strong. Instead, try challenging yourself to only buy fabric for a particular project – if you find the temptation is hard to resist, consider treating yourself to a fancy coffee as a reward for being so restrained.

Choose organic

Look out for fabrics labelled with the Global Organic Textile Standard certification. Organic fabric production uses no chemicals, pesticides or fertilisers to protect local habitats and uses less water than traditional fabric production which in turn limits soil erosion and preserves soil quality for future crops.

This colourful quilt was made from one single Jelly Roll that had been languishing unused for over a year.

Reuse

Once you've reduced your consumption, it's time to start reusing what you already have. Quilters have long been advocates of making the most of left-over fabric and repurposing old clothes and sheets to make something new and functional yet still aesthetically pleasing.

Sew scrappy

Very few quilt projects produce absolutely no scraps or left-over cuts of fabric that can't be repurposed in a new block or quilt. Just because you're using leftovers doesn't mean you can't produce a beautiful quilt: scrappy sewing is incredibly popular among modern quilters who love the fun and eclectic aesthetic built around bold and bright scraps combined in new and exciting ways. Many quilting guilds host fabric and scrap swaps at their meet-ups, which are great places to share fabrics you no longer want.

Even seemingly mismatched scraps can combine to create something beautiful from fabric that would otherwise be thrown away.

Repurpose old fabric

From old work shirts to vintage sheets, you may have more fabric available than you initially realised. Deconstructing a cotton shirt produces a surprisingly large amount of 'new' fabric perfect for making quilt blocks and old sheets are perfect for backing quilts without having to piece fabric to the required size. If you don't happen to have a handy pile of hand-me-down sheets available, charity shops can be a great source of affordable second-hand materials.

The popularity of this approach to reducing the environmental impact of quilting was celebrated in 2023 by the Festival of Quilts' introduction of a new competition category for sustainable quilts made from reused materials. They define a sustainable quilt as one made with minimal negative environmental impact and at least 75 per cent reused fabric.

Recycle

Some scraps and offcuts just can't be reused, either because they are too small or because they're no longer in a state suitable for sewing. If this is the case, try one of the following options:

- Use tiny scraps for stuffing cushions and toys.
- Check if your local recycling centre accepts scrap fabric and thread trimmings. If not, there are various online schemes that accept posted scraps.
- If your fabric is made purely of natural fibres, you can compost small scraps.
- Talk to your local charity shop. Some are paid to fill rag bags with unusable fabrics/clothes and may be happy to add your scraps.
- Try another craft. Tiny offcuts of fabric can make a great addition to a collage or a cute Christmas garland for a doll's house.

LET'S GO!

People quilt for lots of reasons. From the simple utility of wanting a warming quilt, to wanting a fun and creative outlet, to reducing stress and anxiety through the calming motions of working with your hands – whatever your reason, hopefully this book will aid you on your journey.

You can work through this book in order, making all the suggested blocks and quilts as you go, or you can go freestyle and dip in and out as you want – there are no quilt police looking over your shoulder telling you how to use this book. Even if you're making your first ever quilt, you don't have to start with the Modern Sampler quilt pattern – start with whichever you want to make the most. One or two of the quilt patterns are a little more advanced, but if you go slowly and refer to the relevant blocks and techniques you will be able to make any quilt you wish to.

CHAPTER 2

QUILTER'S DICTIONARY

When you first step into the world of quilting it can feel a little like stepping off an aeroplane in a foreign country and being surrounded by a completely alien language. This dictionary includes the most commonly used quilting terms, tools and techniques and will act as your guide as you work through this book and beyond.

BACKING   The fabric used on the back or reverse of a quilt.

BASTING   Used interchangeably with tacking, basting is the process of temporarily securing the three layers of your quilt sandwich ready for quilting.

BATTING   Used interchangeably with wadding, batting is the hidden middle layer of a quilt that adds warmth and stability and determines the thickness of the finished quilt. Commonly made from cotton, bamboo, wool or polyester, each brand will have a recommended maximum space between quilting lines to prevent the fibres coming apart when washed.

BEARDING   The effect of batting fibres passing through to the top of a quilt, leaving a pale fuzz across the surface.

BETWEENS   *See* Quilting needle.

BIAS   The grain of fabric 45 degrees to the warp and weft threads. It has the greatest stretch of any woven fabric grain.

BIAS BINDING   Binding that is cut on the bias, giving it greater flexibility for curved or scalloped quilt edges.

BIAS TAPE MAKER   A device that helps easily make single-fold binding in a set width.

BIG BLOCK QUILTS   A quilt made of large blocks (typically 9–12in plus) to create a high-impact and generally fast-to-assemble quilt top.

BIG STITCH BINDING   Binding that is sewn down using the big stitch hand-quilting technique for a decorative finish.

BIG STITCH QUILTING   A hand-quilting technique that uses thick quilting or embroidery threads to make large decorative stitches.

BINDING   A long strip of fabric which is sewn over the edges of a trimmed quilt as a border to hide and secure the raw edges. Typically, the binding strip is attached to one side of the quilt before being wrapped around the edge to the other side and stitched down.

BINDING CLIPS   Also known by the brand name Wonder Clips, these are small plastic clips used when attaching binding to hold the layers in place while moving through your machine or hand stitching in place.

BLIND STITCH   Also known as a slip stitch or invisible stitch, a blind stitch is used when you want your stitches to be hidden when joining fabrics.

BLOCK   A pieced section of patchwork that is joined with other blocks to form a quilt top. Can be made from smaller sub-blocks.

BOBBIN   A small plastic or metal cylinder with a flared top and bottom used to hold and feed the bottom thread when machine stitching.

BOBBIN CHICKEN   The act of trying to sew to the end of a seam or quilting line before the bobbin thread runs out.

BURYING THREADS   The process of securing and hiding threads when stopping or starting a quilting line in the middle of your quilt (used in both machine and hand quilting).

CHAIN PIECING   The process of sewing prepared pieces of fabric continuously without stopping to cut your threads between blocks.

CHARM PACK   A small pre-cut of fabric measuring 5 × 5in. Often sold in packs including samples from a whole fabric collection, they are useful for scrappy-look quilts or when you only need a little of a lot of different fabrics (for example English Paper Piecing).

COURTHOUSE STEPS   A classic quilt block made by adding strips to opposite sides of a central square.

CREWEL NEEDLE   *See* Embroidery needle.

CROSS GRAIN   The grain of fabric running perpendicular to the selvedge and parallel to the weft threads.

CUTTING MAT   A durable mat for cutting fabric and trimming blocks.

D9P   Disappearing Nine-Patch, a classic pieced quilt block.

DOG EARS   The long points that extend beyond the seam allowance once a block is pieced and pressed.

DOMESTIC MACHINE   A sewing machine designed for the myriad of projects undertaken by home sewists.

DOMESTIC QUILTING   The process of using a domestic machine to quilt your quilt.

DOUBLE-FOLD BINDING   A type of binding where two layers of fabric cover the edge of the quilt.

DRUNKARD'S PATH   A common name for a classic quarter circle quilt block.

DUAL FEED FOOT   *See* Walking foot.

ECHO QUILTING   Quilting lines that follow the edge of a shape and echo like ripples in a pond.

EDGE-TO-EDGE QUILTING   A quilting design that goes continuously from edge to edge of a quilt, removing the need to bury threads.

EMBROIDERY NEEDLE   With a slightly elongated eye, embroidery needles allow for multiple strands of thread or thicker threads to pass through easily and are well suited to big stitch hand quilting.

EMBROIDERY SCISSORS   Small, sharp scissors designed for cutting loose threads.

ENGLISH PAPER PIECING (EPP)   A traditional hand-piecing technique that dates back to the 1700s. Fabric is folded around paper templates to create crisp and precise shapes before later removing the papers.

EVEN FEED FOOT   *See* Walking foot.

EYE   The hole in a sewing needle through which thread moves while stitching.

FABRIC PEN   A temporary marker to show cutting, stitching or quilting lines. Most commonly they are water, air or heat erasable.

FABRIC SCISSORS   Scissors with extremely sharp blades made specifically for cutting fabric. Typically, they measure 8¼in from handle to tip and should never be used for paper or other materials to avoid blunting the blades.

FACING   A method of binding that gives a quilt a crisp edge with no visual border by turning the edge to the back of the quilt.

FAT EIGHTH (F8)   A small cut of fabric made by cutting a fat quarter in half again. If cutting down from a yard (typical in the US) the fat eighth will measure 9 × 21in. If cutting down from a metre (typical in the UK and Europe) it will measure 9¾ × 21in.

FAT QUARTER (FQ)   The most commonly used cut of quilting cotton made by cutting a yard or metre into four squares. If cutting a half yard the fat quarter will measure 18 × 21in. If cutting a metre the FQ will measure 19½ × 21in.

FAT SIXTEENTH (F16)   A small cut of fabric made by cutting a fat eighth in half again. If cutting down from a yard the fat sixteenth will measure 9 × 10½in. If cutting down from a metre it will measure 9¾ × 10½in.

FEED DOGS   The teeth under your sewing machine's presser foot that help to move the fabric through at an even rate.

FINGER PRESSING   Using the heat and pressure from your fingers to press a seam or fold into fabric instead of an iron. Often used to mark the middle of a block or piece of fabric.

FINISHED SIZE   The size of a finished block or quilt when the seam allowance is taken away.

FLIMSY   Another name for a finished quilt top.

FLYING GEESE   The common name for a 2:1 rectangle block containing a triangle like the V shape made by a flock of geese in flight. It is twice as wide as it is high.

FOUNDATION PAPER PIECING (FPP)   A machine stitching technique used to create precise and detailed shapes. Fabric is sewn to paper templates to create intricate shapes with ease while avoiding potentially tricky Y or partial seams (the paper is later removed).

FRAME   A large structure that holds the layers of your quilt sandwich in position while you quilt. Often used for hand quilting large quilts, they are also used in long arm quilting.

FREE-MOTION QUILTING (FMQ)   The technique of quilting with lowered feed dogs so that you can move the quilt freely in all directions and control stitch length yourself.

FUSSY CUTTING   Also called meticulous cutting or precision cutting, fussy cutting is the careful cutting of fabric to include a specific section or motif. This technique can be used to great effect in creating kaleidoscopes and is very popular in English Paper Piecing.

GLUE BASTING   Using a temporary fabric adhesive spray to baste your quilt sandwich.

GRAIN   The orientation of the warp and weft threads in a woven fabric (such as quilting cotton).

HALF-RECTANGLE TRIANGLE (HRT)   A common rectangular quilt block (usually in a 2:1 ratio) formed of two right-angled triangles.

HALF-SQUARE TRIANGLE (HST)   A very common square quilt block formed of two right-angled triangles.

HAND QUILTING   The process of quilting a quilt by hand.

HANGING SLEEVE   A long tube attached to the back of a quilt to facilitate hanging and display. The standard width required by most quilt shows is approximately 4–5in.

HERA MARKER   A piece of hard plastic or wood with a rounded edge used to create light crease lines to guide you while quilting. Sometimes called a sewing crease marker.

INSET CIRCLES   The process of inserting a whole circle into a quilt or block.

INVISIBLE STITCH   *See* Blind stitch.

JELLY ROLL   A pre-cut of fabric measuring 2½ × WOFin (width of fabric in inches). Often sold in rolled packs including samples from a whole fabric collection. Jelly Roll is a brand name for this fabric cut; other brand names include Roll Up, Rolie Polie and Strip Sets.

LAYER CAKE   A pre-cut of fabric measuring 10 × 10in. Often sold in packs including samples from a whole fabric collection.

LEADER   A small scrap of fabric placed under the needle at the beginning of machine sewing to prevent thread tangles when stitching blocks together.

LOCAL QUILT SHOP (LQS)   A term used for independent fabric and haberdashery shops that specialise in quilting fabric, threads and accessories. They may not be truly local as many sell online as well as in bricks-and-mortar stores.

LOFT   The weight or thickness of batting that determines the overall puffiness of your quilt.

LOG CABIN   A classic quilt block made by adding strips in a clockwise direction around a central square.

LONG ARM MACHINE   A specialist quilting machine consisting of a sewing machine head and large frame that can be computerised or manually operated.

LONG ARM QUILTING   The process of using a long arm machine to quilt your quilt sandwich.

LONG QUARTER (LQ)   A cut of fabric made by cutting a yard or metre into four long rectangles. If cutting a half yard the long quarter will measure 9 × WOFin. If cutting a metre the long quarter will measure 9¾ × WOFin.

LOW VOLUME FABRIC   Pale fabrics with cream or neutral backgrounds and a subtle design. The design will usually be printed in a colour the same or similar to the background fabric.

MACHINE QUILTING   The process of quilting your quilt with a domestic machine.

MACHINE STITCHING   The process of sewing with a machine. Top and bottom (bobbin) thread are used by a machine to create even and regular stitches.

METICULOUS CUTTING   *See* Fussy cutting.

MILLINERS' NEEDLES   A needle with a longer length, milliners' needles are popular with many English Paper Piecing enthusiasts.

MITRED CORNER   A 90-degree corner where two edges meet at a 45-degree angle. Usually used to create crisp and sharp corners when binding or adding borders to a quilt.

MODERN QUILTING   The term modern quilting encompasses a huge range of quilting styles which have been inspired by modern design principles, colours and fabrics.

NESTING SEAMS   The process of pressing adjoining seams in opposite directions so that they fit snugly together when sewn together and give crisp corners or points.

NO-WASTE FLYING GEESE   A method of making multiple Flying Geese blocks at a time that involves no excess discarded fabric. Sometimes called four-at-a-time Flying Geese.

NOTIONS   These are the various extra supplies needed to complete a quilt. Examples include thread, needles and scissors.

ON POINT   A square block set diagonally (standing on its 'point') so that it represents a diamond shape.

ONE PATCH QUILT   A quilt made with one block shape repeated throughout.

ORANGE PEEL   A common quilt block made by sewing two curved seams from corner to corner of a square to create a leaf or petal shape in the centre of the block.

PANTOGRAPH   Also called a panto, a pantograph is a continuous line edge-to-edge quilting design that covers the entire quilt top. Typically used to guide complex designs with many curves or sharp angles.

PARTIAL SEAMS   A partial seam is used when a block has unevenly placed pieces that cannot be joined along a straight line.

PATCHWORK   The traditional name for piecing fabric together to make a quilt top. These days the term is often used interchangeably with quilting, with many sewists referring to this piecing stage as quilting.

PIECING   The process of joining fabric pieces together by either machine or hand to make a larger piece.

PIN BASTING   Using curved safety pins to baste your quilt sandwich.

PRE-CUT   A pre-cut piece of fabric in a standardised size, typically available in bundles or as packs.

PRECISION CUTTING   *See* Fussy cutting.

PRESSER FOOT   A sewing machine attachment used to hold fabric flat as it is fed through the machine.

PRESSING   The process of setting the fabric of your seam allowance either to one side or open to help merge your stitches into the fabric and create permanent folds in the fabric along the seam.

QUARTER-INCH FOOT   Also known as a quilting foot, a quarter-inch foot is a specialist presser foot for domestic machines that has a guide for placing your fabric to sew precise ¼in seams. It is often included with the supplies for more expensive machines but can easily be bought as an optional extra for most domestic machines.

QUARTER-SQUARE TRIANGLE (QST)   A common square quilt block formed of four right-angled triangles arranged in an X shape.

QUICK UNPICK   *See* Seam ripper.

QUILT   A multi-layered textile made of two layers of fabric either side of a layer of batting and secured by stitching (quilting) through all three layers. Typically, it has a bound edge.

QUILT DESIGN   The arrangement of fabric, colour or blocks to form a specific overall design. Not to be confused with Quilting Design.

QUILT MARKING   The process of marking your quilting lines to act as a guide when quilting.

QUILT PATTERN   Instructions on how to make a specific quilt design, typically including fabric requirements, piecing and construction instructions.

QUILT SANDWICH   The three layers of a quilt when assembled ready for basting: the quilt top, the batting and the backing.

QUILT TOP   The front or top layer of a quilt, it can be pieced or a single wholecloth piece of fabric.

QUILTING FOOT *See* Quarter-inch foot.

QUILTING COTTON A medium-weight fabric made using 100 per cent cotton and a plain weave that is hard-wearing and stable to sew with.

QUILTING DESIGN The line pattern created by stitching the quilt sandwich together either by machine or by hand. Not to be confused with Quilt Design.

QUILTING HOOP A large hoop that holds the layers of your quilt sandwich in position while you hand quilt. Similar in style to embroidery hoops, they have a larger depth of ¾–1in to accommodate the thicker and heavier layers of a quilt.

QUILTING NEEDLES A shorter needle, a quilting needle is designed to allow small and precise stitches when hand quilting with fine thread.

QUILTING PINS Sharp, straight pins with a stopper on one end designed to keep fabric together and aligned while being sewn.

RIGHT SIDE The top or nice side of printed fabric. The right side is generally the side you want to show off in your quilt.

RIGHT SIDES TOGETHER (RST) Placing the right sides of your fabric together in preparation for sewing a seam.

ROTARY CUTTER A tool for cutting fabric consisting of a handle and replaceable circular blade resembling a pizza cutter.

ROW When assembling a quilt top, blocks are commonly sewn together in long rows and then joined along the long seams for easier assembly.

RULERS Thick acrylic rulers marked at varying size increments to help you make precise measurements and accurate cuts. They come in various shapes, for example squares, rectangles and equilateral triangles among others.

SAMPLER QUILT A quilt made using a variety of blocks and techniques, usually as a skill builder.

SASHING Strips of fabric used to separate pieced blocks when joining your quilt top.

SCANT ¼IN A seam sewn a thread's width smaller than a standard ¼in to allow for greater accuracy when piecing.

SCRAPPY QUILTING The practice of making a quilt or quilts just from scraps and other leftover pieces of fabric.

SCRAPS The leftover pieces of fabric from making a quilt. These scraps are often saved to be repurposed.

SCRIM A light layer of woven fibres added to some battings to act as a stabiliser and hold the fibres together while quilting. Batting with scrim often allows for a larger spacing of your quilting lines.

SEAM ALLOWANCE The space between the cut edge of your fabric and the stitched line. Unless a pattern specifies otherwise, the standard quilting seam size is ¼in.

SEAM RIPPER Also called a quick unpick, a seam ripper is a small tool that has a sharp pointed end that will cut and unpick stitches quickly.

SEAM ROLLER A small roller used to temporarily press seams without the need for a hot iron. This is especially useful in Foundation Paper Piecing.

SELVEDGE The finished edges of woven fabric created during the weaving process. They often have small holes from the printing process, and may have information about the fabric maker/designer. They are usually discarded – however, increasingly selvedges are now being designed in such a way that they can be used to add an interesting extra design element to your quilt.

SEWING CREASE MARKER *See* Hera marker.

SHARPS A short- to medium-length needle, sharps are a good all-purpose needle suited to a wide range of hand-sewing.

SIMPLE KNOT   A basic overhand knot, a simple knot is used to secure thread ends before burying.

SINGLE-FOLD BINDING   A type of binding where only one layer of fabric covers the edge of the quilt.

SLICE AND STITCH   A simple technique for creating complex-looking block designs where an assembled block is cut up, rearranged and sewn back together. Most commonly used for the Disappearing Nine-Patch block.

SLIP STITCH   *See* Blind stitch.

SNIPS   *See* Embroidery scissors.

SQUARING UP   The process of trimming your quilt corners to 90 degrees ready for binding or aligning a straight edge on your fabric to prepare it for cutting into strips or pieces.

STASH   A colloquial term for the collection of fabric every quilter inevitably accumulates.

STASH BUSTING   Sewing a quilt using only fabric from your collection to reduce the size of your collection.

STENCIL   A template used to mark quilting designs on a quilt top, usually made from a thin acetate with the design cut out.

STILETTO   A tool with a tapered end used to hold fabric with accuracy where it may be difficult to safely hold with your fingers.

STITCH-IN-THE-DITCH QUILTING   A quilting design that entails sewing along the seam lines of the quilt top to hide the quilting stitches and emphasise your piecing.

STITCHING PLATE   A metal plate that sits below the needle and presser foot on a sewing machine. Small openings in the plate allow the bobbin thread to come out, the feed dogs to rise and the needle to move through.

STRAIGHT GRAIN   The grain of fabric running parallel to the selvedge and warp threads.

STRAIGHT-LINE QUILTING   Quilting designs that only use straight lines, including those that have turns and pivots.

STRAW NEEDLES   *See* Milliners' needles.

STRIP PIECING   The process of joining strips of fabric before cutting them into individual quilt blocks.

SUB-BLOCK   For blocks with multiple stages of construction, a sub-block is a smaller pieced unit that will become part of the overall whole.

TACKING   *See* Basting.

TAILOR'S CHALK   A hard chalk used to temporarily mark fabric.

TEMPLATES   A template used to mark quilting designs on a quilt top, usually made from a thick acrylic, *OR* A template used to trace block shapes for EPP (English Paper Piecing).

THIMBLE   A protective cover worn over the fingertip to protect from the sharpness of a needle while hand stitching.

THREAD BASTING   Using large, loose stitches to baste your quilt sandwich.

THREAD WEIGHT   The thickness of a thread.

THROAT   The space in a sewing machine between the needle and the vertical arm on the right of the machine.

TRADITIONAL QUILTING   Traditional quilting often uses repeated shapes, classic quilt blocks, neutral backgrounds and small-scale prints.

TRIMMING   The process of trimming excess backing and batting from a finished quilt to prepare it for binding, *OR* The process of trimming an oversized block to the required size.

UNFINISHED OBJECT (UFO)   A colloquial term for a long-term WIP (work in progress).

UNFINISHED SIZE   The size of a block including the seam allowance, generally ½in larger in each dimension than the finished size.

WADDING   *See* Batting.

WALKING FOOT   Also known as a dual feed or even feed foot, a walking foot is a specialist presser foot for domestic machines that provides a second set of feed dogs to help feed the multiple layers of a quilt through your machine at an even rate and without slippage between layers.

WALKING-FOOT QUILTING   Straight-line machine quilting using a walking foot.

WARP   The threads that run vertically down woven fabric parallel to the selvedge.

WEB PIECING   A method of chain-piecing multiple blocks into rows.

WEFT   The threads that run horizontally across woven fabric perpendicular to the selvedge.

WHIPSTITCH   The most common joining stitch in English Paper Piecing where the needle and thread are passed through the fabric in a continuous circle to create a row of looped stitches around the edge of the fabric.

WHITE ON WHITE (WOW)   White fabric with a white pattern printed on it for added low volume visual interest.

WHOLECLOTH QUILT   A quilt made using a single piece of fabric as the top instead of a pieced quilt top.

WIDTH OF FABRIC (WOF)   The useable width between the selvedges. For quilting cotton this is typically 42in once the selvedges have been removed.

WONDER CLIPS   *See* Binding clips.

WORK IN PROGRESS (WIP)   An unfinished quilt that is still in progress.

WRONG SIDE   The reverse of a printed fabric. The wrong side is the side you generally want to hide inside the quilt.

WRONG SIDES TOGETHER (WST)   Placing the wrong sides of your fabric together in preparation for sewing.

Y SEAM   When three or more seams join but do not form a right angle.

YARDAGE   The length of fabric required when measured parallel to the selvedge. This term can also refer to length when cutting by the metre so check the unit of sale before ordering.

YARN DYED FABRIC   A fabric pattern or colour which has been created by using dyed fibres instead of printing.

CHAPTER 3

MATERIALS AND EQUIPMENT

When dipping your toe into the exciting world of quilting, it can be easy to feel overwhelmed by all the different materials and equipment on offer – and how much they all cost! This chapter will walk you through which tools really are essential and which are nice-to-haves, what to look out for when shopping for new tools, how to choose the right needle and thread for your project and explain exactly what a fat quarter is.

These are not intended to be exhaustive checklists of what to buy but rather the starting point for a lifetime of exploration and the slow gathering of tools that truly add value to and aid your quilting practice. Sewing and quilting should be open to all. However, not every tool is suited for every quilter, so the chapter finishes with some general hints and tips for adapting to different accessibility needs.

TOOLS

Quilters often tout certain tools as 'essential' and claim that they 'couldn't live without them' but it is best to start with a small core of tools and then slowly add to your collection as your quilting practice evolves and your budget allows. There are lots of tools that can make quilting easier but not every quilter will find every tool helpful. For example, someone who loves the precision and process of Foundation Paper Piecing (FPP) may have different needs to someone who prefers a more classic piecing approach, so take time to consider each purchase.

Essential starter kit

The actual list of true essentials is quite limited and (barring the sewing machine) doesn't have to break the bank when you're first starting out. Using just these basics, you will be able to enjoy any quilting project you set your mind to.

Sewing machine

While it is more than possible to sew a quilt entirely by hand – as generations of quilters going back centuries have proven – in the twenty-first century most quilters like to do at least some sewing by machine. A domestic sewing machine should last years with the proper care, so it is worth doing your research about different makes and models and ideally trying out any shortlisted machines before purchasing.

Things to consider when buying a sewing machine:
- Do you want a mechanical or computerised machine? Mechanical machines do not have display screens and stitch width and length are manually set by adjusting dials. Generally considered the more basic type, they are excellent workhorse machines and are easy to maintain as they lack electronic parts. Computerised machines typically have a lot more functions than mechanical machines and it is easier to adjust stitches more precisely. Usually offering a large range of decorative stitch options as well as standard straight stitches, many modern machines offer automatic needle threaders, thread cutters, automatic presser foot position detection and more. They are however often more expensive than mechanical machines due to the reliance on technology and can be trickier to maintain. They also may eventually become obsolete as manufacturers eventually no longer support repair.
- Which presser feet are included? You will likely want to invest in a ¼in quilter's foot and a walking foot if they are not included, so remember to factor that into the total cost.
- How many different stitch types are there? Straight stitch machines can be very effective for quilting but exclude the option of decorative or zig zag stitches. Before being drawn in by a huge variety of stitches, consider how many you are likely to use – there is no point paying for more if you aren't going to use them.

- How wide is the throat space (the space between the needle and the vertical arm on the right of the machine)? Large quilts can be quilted on standard small-throated machines, although it is more difficult to manoeuvre the quilt sandwich through evenly without creating puckers. The larger the throat space, the easier it is to manoeuvre big quilts through.
- How big and heavy is the machine? If the machine will be left out or moved only occasionally, a larger, heavier machine usually isn't a problem, while if it will be moved around a lot or travel to other locations (for example, sewing days), a lighter, smaller machine may be more suitable.
- What is the availability of spare parts and servicing for your chosen model in your area? There is nothing worse than being stopped mid-project and having to wait for weeks for a non-local service to fix a problem.
- Is there the option to add a knee lift? Common in higher-end machines, a knee lift lets you raise the presser foot without moving your hands and gives you more control over the fabric. It can also be very helpful as an accessibility aid.

Caring for your sewing machine:
- Clean under the stitching plate regularly, ideally after finishing each quilt as batting fluff can build up quickly and cause skipped stitches.
- Have it serviced annually if using it regularly, or every two to three years if used only occasionally. By smoothing out any kinks before they become big problems you will help extend the life of your machine by several years and save money in the long run.
- Check any maintenance requirements specific to your machine brand and model. For example, some machines will need regular oiling while others should never be oiled.
- If it is not in regular use, keep it covered to prevent dust accumulating in the machinery.

45mm rotary cutter

When cutting fabric, trimming blocks and squaring up quilts, a rotary cutter is the quilter's best friend. Trying to cut all the fabric needed for a quilt and accurately trim blocks with fabric scissors is such a slow and time-consuming process that a 45mm rotary cutter is an essential tool for all quilters. Based on the same principle as a pizza cutter, a rotary cutter can easily and accurately cut through multiple layers of fabric at once and give smooth edges to longer cuts.

Things to look out for when shopping:
- When it comes to handle shape for a rotary cutter, there are now quite a few different options designed to reduce wrist fatigue so spend some time thinking about which shape you'll find most comfortable to use and try out a few different options if you can.
- The blade cover should be quick and easy to open and close one-handed.
- Cutting lots of fabric can wear down cutting blades relatively quickly so the ability to replace the blades is a must. The cost of replacement blades is also something to take into consideration and whether only branded blades will fit or if off-brand options are available.
- Olfa and Fiskars are usually considered to be the leading brands of rotary cutters. While low-budget options are fine for most quilting essentials, it is worth spending a little bit more, if possible, on a reputable rotary cutter brand rather than getting a craft store's own brand version, as they often last much longer and run more smoothly over the long term.

Caring for your rotary cutter:
- Change the blade regularly to not only ensure smooth sharp cuts in your fabric but also reduce wrist and hand fatigue when spending a long time cutting. Quilters vary wildly in their views of how often a blade should be changed, but there is a consensus that if you think it's been a while, it probably needs changing. A good rule of thumb is to change it after every couple of projects or any very intensive fabric cutting sessions.
- Clean the area around the blade regularly as small threads and fluff can build up in the little crevices. This can be easily done by temporarily removing the blade and wiping it down before replacing the blade.

Cutting mat

A cutting mat is the bread to the rotary cutter's butter, the perfect partner in crime. Without a cutting mat, a rotary cutter will soon leave your tables marked and scratched beyond repair. While there is a place for all sizes of cutting mat from A5 to A0, the best starting size is arguably A3. This is large enough to trim the long edge of a fat quarter and is also big enough to trim the most common sizes of quilt blocks.

Things to look out for when shopping:
- A self-healing surface is a must in any cutting mat. While cutting mats do not self-heal forever and will eventually need to be replaced, a self-healing surface extends the life of the mat significantly.
- Measurements should be shown in inches and clearly indicate the inch, half-inch and quarter-inch intervals.

Caring for your cutting mat:

- Do not roll or bend them or leave them in the sun or by a heater, as these can permanently misshape them.
- To extend its life, clean your mat regularly using soapy water and dry thoroughly before using again.

6½ × 24in quilting ruler

There are almost as many different quilting rulers as there are quilters, but when starting out you'll want to get a 6½ × 24in ruler. This size will allow for easy squaring up of fat quarters, larger quilt blocks and quilted tops.

Things to look out for when shopping:

- Make sure the measurements are shown in inches and show the inch, half-inch, quarter-inch and ideally eighth-inch intervals clearly.
- Check that there are 45-degree, 60-degree and 30-degree angle marks to help with trimming blocks and cutting triangles.
- It should be made of a sturdy clear acrylic that is roughly ¼in thick without too much flexibility, so it will hold up to a rotary cutter running against it repeatedly.
- Ensure that the markings will show up against a wide variety of fabric colours and prints but are not so brightly marked that they will overly obscure or distract when measuring and cutting.

Caring for your quilting rulers:

- Do not bend them as they can snap if too much force is applied.
- Pay attention to the corners when using a rotary cutter to avoid accidentally chipping away at the acrylic.
- Keep them away from basting spray or other adhesives to avoid residue build-up that can transfer to your fabric.

Iron

There is no need to go out and buy a specialised sewing iron to press your projects: a standard household iron does the job perfectly.

Things to look out for if you do need to buy an iron:

- A good-length power cable that will allow freedom of movement over a wide area, for example when pressing quilt backs or long seams.
- The option to turn the steam on and off as the moisture can warp and distort fabric. As a positive, this means that you can reshape blocks slightly to make squaring up a bit easier. As a negative, it can make initially square blocks go askew during pressing.
- Ideally a good pressing iron has some weight behind it to help with the pressing process. However, this can strain your hands and wrists when pressing lots of blocks at once so ensure that you can lift it up and down over and over without causing too much physical strain.
- A nice-to-have is an automatic 'off' setting in case you leave it on by accident or aren't using it for a long time, but this is not essential.

Caring for your iron:

- *If using the steam function, regularly de-scale your iron to prevent limescale build-up. This build-up can then be expelled onto your fabric, especially if you live in a hard water area.*
- *Clean any residue from the surface of the iron as soon as it becomes apparent using a soft non-abrasive cloth and warm soapy water.*

Embroidery scissors

Small embroidery scissors should be kept close to hand for trimming loose threads when piecing and quilting.

Things to look out for when shopping:
- Embroidery scissors (or snips) should be small so that they are easy to pick up and put down as needed.
- There are a variety of shapes of embroidery scissors from the simple small scissors to squeezable snips to the classic stork and beyond, so consider which shape you find most comfortable to use and easy to quickly pick up by trying out a few different styles.

Caring for your embroidery scissors:
- Only use them for trimming threads to keep the blades sharp – fabric will dull them and reduce their lifespan.

Straight pins

A true sewing essential, straight pins have an almost limitless number of uses in quilting, from simply holding fabric together to marking the top of a block to helping align seam junctions perfectly.

Things to look out for when shopping:
- A minimum length of around 1½–2in to accommodate pinning through multiple layers of fabric.
- Quilting straight pins have a 'head'; a small ball made of either plastic or glass, to help you see them when sewing. When choosing between glass and plastic heads consider whether you are likely to iron over your pins (which would melt plastic heads).
- The thickness of quilting straight pins is slightly greater than fine dressmaking pins, which are designed for very fine fabrics such as silk. Cotton has a looser weave that bounces back from pinning much more easily.

Curved safety pins

The most popular method of basting a quilt sandwich uses curved safety pins (not standard safety pins). These pins can also be used for attaching labels to fabric, holding a pile of blocks together or anything else that comes to mind.

Things to look out for when shopping:
- When used for basting, you will likely need more than you think, especially when making large quilts. Start out with a couple of medium-sized packs and then add as you need.
- The pins should be reasonably substantial and not too flimsy to the touch so they can securely hold multiple layers of fabric and batting without popping open.

Seam ripper

While it isn't anyone's favourite tool, a seam ripper (also called a quick unpick) is an essential. A small tool that has a sharp pointed end that will cut and unpick stitches quickly, it makes fixing mistakes relatively quick and painless. Often a basic seam ripper will be included with your sewing machine, but if not, it is worth purchasing one before you need it.

Things to look out for when shopping:
- Look for an ergonomic handle – it will be easier to hold and use, as well as making unpicking slightly less frustrating.
- Can the blade be replaced? Eventually the blade will wear down (or you may accidentally snap the pointed end) and it may need replacing.

Useful tools

Once you've tried your hand at quilting and decided it's the hobby for you (and why wouldn't you?), you'll probably want to invest in a few tools that, while not technically essential, most quilters find themselves purchasing as they help make piecing and quilting much easier.

¼in quilting foot

If you only buy one thing from this section, a ¼in quilting foot should be the one. This simple but powerful piece of equipment is the most highly recommended bit of extra kit by virtually every quilter for one simple reason: it makes sewing an accurate ¼in seam a breeze. Simply line the edge of your fabric up with the guide and stitch away.

Things to look out for when shopping:
- Make sure that the foot you buy is compatible with your machine make and model. Not every accessory by a single manufacturer will work with every machine they make so always check before purchasing.
- Check if you need to change settings or needle position on your machine before using the foot for the first time to avoid accidentally sewing seams that are either too wide or too narrow.

6½ × 6½in quilting ruler

While the 6½ × 24in quilting ruler is great for longer cuts, it can be a little unwieldy when it comes to trimming smaller quilt blocks. A 6½ × 6½in square ruler is easier to move around when trimming and squaring up smaller blocks.

As with the larger ruler, look out for the following when shopping:

- Make sure the measurements are shown in inches.
- Check there are 45-degree, 60-degree and 30-degree angle marks.
- Ensure it is made of sturdy, clear acrylic.
- Markings that will show up against a wide variety of fabric colours and prints.

Walking foot

A quilter's best friend, a walking foot (also known as a dual-feed foot or even-feed foot) has integrated feed dogs to help move the layers of a quilt sandwich through your machine evenly while minimising slippage between layers. When quilting your pieced quilt top, a walking foot reduces the occurrence of little puckers and tucks.

Things to look out for when shopping:

- Make sure that the foot you buy is compatible with your machine make and model.
- Consider buying the brand version rather than an off-brand compatible version as they are typically better quality and last significantly longer without problems.

Basting spray

Basting spray is a temporary adhesive spray used to hold fabric securely in place for a short period of time. Ideal for small quilts and projects that will be quilted soon, basting spray can speed up the basting process significantly. Be careful to only use it in a well-ventilated area and avoid altogether if you have respiratory problems.

Things to look out for when shopping:

- Make sure that the spray is fabric safe and temporary.
- Check the removal instructions – will the spray wash out easily or does it need a specific treatment?

Removable fabric marker

A handy and often underrated tool, a removable fabric marker adds a lot of value to your sewing toolkit. Used to mark sewing lines, help line up sashing, label blocks and more, they have many uses. While there is a strong element of personal preference to which you'll find yourself using most often, some options will be better suited to certain project types than others.

WATER REMOVABLE PEN

- Positives:
  - Easy to draw with.
- Negatives:
  - While it is possible to find these in multiple colours, by far the most common is blue which does not show up well against all fabric colours.
  - You must thoroughly rinse the finished project, which can take away from the crispness of a freshly finished art quilt or display piece.
- Recommended for:
  - Projects that will be washed before use.

AIR ERASABLE PEN

- Positives:
  - Usually vanishes without a trace.
  - Easy to draw with.
- Negatives:
  - Vanishes within a few hours so it is not suitable for marking up longer-term projects or anything that will be left overnight.
  - Colour range is limited and does not work with all fabric colours.
- Recommended for:
  - Quick projects where you don't want to worry about remembering to remove your lines.

Binding clips

Also known by the brand name Wonder Clips, these are small plastic clips used to hold layers of fabric in place while attaching binding to a quilt. That is far from their only use, however. They can also be used to attach labels to fabric, hold a pile of blocks or cut fabric together, quickly show the correct orientation of a block or help you align seam junctions perfectly.

Things to look out for when shopping:
- Start out with a couple of packs and then add more as you need them as you are likely to need quite a few when used for binding.
- Binding clips should feel substantial and not too flimsy to the touch. They need to securely hold multiple layers of fabric and batting without snapping open or falling apart after just a few uses.

HEAT ERASABLE PEN
- Positives:
  – Quick to remove with a simple sweep of a hot iron.
  – Easy to draw with.
- Negatives:
  – Not all fabrics are compatible so may leave undesirable marks.
  – Can reappear in extreme cold (such as an aeroplane hold) and be very difficult to remove again.
- Recommended for:
  – Interior seam lines and other places where it will not be seen in the finished quilt.

CHALK
- Positives:
  – Stands out well against darker fabrics.
- Negatives:
  – Can be frustrating to remove and require lots of brushing out.
  – Coloured chalk can stain lighter-coloured fabrics.
  – More difficult to draw smooth lines with than some other removable markers.
- Recommended for:
  – Projects that will be cleaned before use.

Thimble

A protective cover worn over the middle fingertip to protect from the sharpness of a needle while hand stitching, a thimble is invaluable to anyone doing significant quantities of hand stitching or who accidentally pricks themselves frequently.

Things to look out for when shopping:
- Thimbles should fit snuggly on your finger to prevent slipping.
- Try as many kinds on as you can to find a comfortable fit. Is the classic metal thimble perfect for you, or does a soft-sided silicon or leather thimble suit you more?
- If you struggle to find a thimble that you can comfortably work with, consider trying adhesive dot thimbles. These are stick-on pads that can be reused a few times and only cover the exact spot on your finger that is most at risk of rogue needle pricks.

Nice-to-haves

These are the tools that give quilters their reputation for being spend happy! Not every quilter will want the tools listed below, or find them useful, but if you're thinking about investing a little bit more or adding a few things to your birthday gift list, these are worth considering.

Wool pressing mat

A thick mat made of felted wool, a pressing mat turns any surface into an ironing board. The wool reflects the heat of an iron back as well as absorbing steam and cushioning stitches to effectively press from both sides at once and give crisper seams. The lightweight portability of a wool mat is perfect for taking to sewing days with friends as well as for anyone with limited sewing space.

Things to look out for when shopping:
- A substantial pad at least ½in thick – any less than this and it won't protect the surface below from the heat of the iron.
- 100 per cent pure wool as synthetic fibres won't provide the same benefits.
- Make sure to choose a size that fits your available space – while it may be tempting to get the biggest possible mat, you'll be surprised at how well you can manage with a smaller mat.

Hera marker

A Hera marker (sometimes called a sewing crease marker) is a piece of hard plastic, wood or similar with a rounded edge used to create creases in your fabric which are then used as a guide to sew along. It is especially great for marking quilting lines without using a removable fabric marker as, despite its name, it is not actually a marker so avoids all their disadvantages. It works even on dark fabric as the crease creates a slight shine to the cotton fibres which reflects the light of your sewing machine. Marked the wrong line or changed your mind? Simply iron out the crease with a little steam to reset the fabric and mark again.

Things to look out for when shopping:
- Clover is generally considered one of the best brands of Hera marker, and popularised the name Hera marker, but an increasing number of independent craftspeople are making handcrafted versions that are also worth trying out.
- The rounded edge shouldn't be too thick or blunt otherwise it will be difficult to create an effective crease that will hold up to the quilt being moved around during quilting. It also shouldn't be too thin as that can damage your fabric; aim for approximately a butter-knife width.

Seam roller

A seam roller does exactly what it says on the tin – it rolls seams. Usually used for pre-pressing seams ahead of pressing with an iron, they are especially great for FPP when you don't want to get up and iron press every seam as you sew it.

Things to look out for when shopping:
- The roller width should be approximately ¾–1½in wide to sufficiently cover both sides of a seam when pressing.
- Look beyond your local haberdashery to a DIY/hardware store for wallpaper seam rollers – they are often more substantial than those designed for sewing.

½in quilting ruler

Available in a variety of lengths, a ½in quilting ruler is just ½in wide and is great for marking ¼in and ½in seam or trimming lines on blocks.

Things to look out for when shopping:
- Make sure the measurements show the quarter-inch and eighth-inch intervals.
- The most common lengths are 6in and 12in so choose the size most helpful to you – do you often draw diagonals across blocks? If so the 12in might be the best fit, while if you use it for smaller piecing the 6in may be sufficient.

Tweezers

Tweezers are ideal for grabbing threads from under a presser foot and for removing papers from FPP blocks.

Things to look out for when shopping:
- An angled tip will give you more manoeuvrability when using.
- Pointed tips will help you pull and hold more precisely.

Add-a-Quarter ruler

Like the ½in quilting ruler, an Add-a-Quarter ruler is designed to make trimming a ¼in seam allowance easier. Using the ¼in wide ledge of the edge of a ruler you simply butt it up against the seam you wish to trim and cut away the excess. It is most often used by Foundation Paper Piecing fans as it is very helpful for quickly trimming down seams as you go.

Things to look out for when shopping:
- The ¼in ledge should be around ⅛in thick – any thicker and you risk it wobbling as you trim.
- As with ½in rulers, the most common sizes are 6in and 12in, so choose based on the size of FPP seams you typically work with.

28mm rotary cutter

A smaller version of the essential 45mm rotary cutter, the 28mm is great for curves and small shapes that need more precision than the larger size can accommodate.

As with the larger rotary cutter, you want to look out for the following when shopping:

- A comfortable handle shape that minimises wrist and hand fatigue.
- The blade cover should be quick and easy to open and close one-handed.
- Replacing the blades should be a simple and safe procedure.

Bias tape maker

Taking away the risk of singed fingertips, a bias tape maker is perfect for easily making single-fold binding – and you don't have to cut on the bias for it to work. Simply feed your joined binding strip through the wide end and press as it comes out of the narrow end – *et voilà*, perfectly pressed binding.

Things to look out for when shopping:

- The size given is not the size of the binding when attached and folded over but rather the width of the binding from fold to fold, in other words, twice the actual finished binding width. For a quilt, ½in finished binding is the most used size so a 1in (25mm) bias tape maker is often the most useful size.

Light box

A light box isn't usually an actual box nowadays, but instead a thin and portable LED device that shines a very bright light when turned on. On the 'only if you really want it' end of the nice-to-have scale, a light box can be helpful when fussy cutting or lining up FPP seams.

Things to look out for when shopping:

- Battery powered vs plug-in – if you're likely to take it out and about to sewing days with you, consider opting for a rechargeable battery-powered model. If it's mainly going to be used at home, plug-in offers a cheaper option.
- Check what brightness settings are available as you may not always want the brightest possible option.

FABRIC

Now that you've got the tools to get started, it's time to get some fabric. Taking a quilter into a fabric shop is akin to taking a small child into a sweet shop. However, unlike a child who is held back by the sense and restraint of their responsible adult, a quilter can buy as much fabric as their heart (or at least their bank account) allows. With bolts neatly stacked in rows like strokable jewels, the possibilities are endless, and it can be hard to choose just a few to take home. A warning should be made here about the hoarding tendencies of quilters: the urge to get 'just one more fat quarter' can be hard to resist and many claim that fabric collecting is an entirely separate hobby to quilting!

At the beginning it can be quite confusing as to where to start in what is a veritable ocean of options: what fabric do you need to make a quilt? Is one cotton the same as another? And what *is* a fat quarter?

Anatomy of a yard of fabric

Depending on where in the world you live, fabric from the bolt may be sold either by the yard or by the metre. Despite this difference in retail unit, it is usually referred to as yardage even when sold by the metre: yardage is calculated as the length of fabric required when measured parallel to the selvedge.

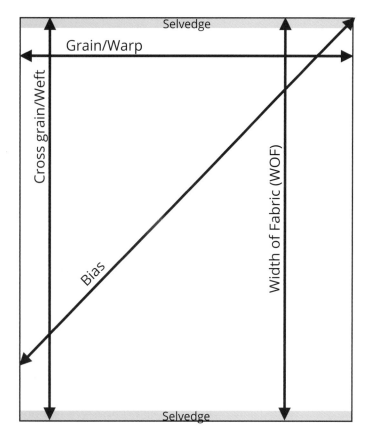

Pre-cuts

Not every project needs large quantities of a single fabric and buying yardage of each different colour or print you need for a project can get very expensive very quickly. Luckily quilters have already thought about this and come up with the more budget-friendly concept of pre-cuts. Pre-cuts are quite simply a pre-cut piece of fabric in a standardised size, typically sold in bundles or as packs.

- **Fat quarter (FQ):** The most common cut of quilting cotton, made by cutting a yard or metre into four squares. If cutting a yard (typical in the US) the FQ will measure 18 × 21in and if cutting a metre (typical in the UK and Europe) the FQ will measure 19½ × 21in.
- **Long quarter (LQ):** A cut of fabric made by cutting a yard or metre into four longways. If cutting a yard the LQ will measure 9 × WOF inch and if cutting a metre the FQ will measure 9¾ × WOF inch.
- **Fat eighth (F8):** A small cut of fabric made by cutting a fat quarter in half again. If cutting down from a yard the F8 will measure 9 × 21in, alternatively if cutting down from a metre it will measure 9¾ × 21in.
- **Fat sixteenth (F16):** A small cut of fabric made by cutting a fat eighth in half again. If cutting down from a yard the F16 will measure 9 × 10½in, alternatively if cutting down from a metre it will measure 9¾ × 10½in.
- **Jelly Roll:** A pre-cut of fabric measuring 2½ × WOF inch. Often sold in rolled packs including samples from a whole fabric collection.
- **Layer cake:** A pre-cut of fabric measuring 10 × 10in. Often sold in packs including samples from a whole fabric collection.
- **Charm pack:** A small pre-cut of fabric measuring 5 × 5in. Often sold in packs including samples from a whole fabric collection, they are useful for scrappy-look quilts or when you only need a little of a lot of different fabrics (for example English Paper Piecing).

- **Warp:** The threads that run vertically down woven fabric parallel to the selvedge.
- **Weft:** The threads that run horizontally across woven fabric perpendicular to the selvedge.
- **Selvedge:** The finished edges of woven fabric created during the weaving process. They often have small holes from the printing process or information about the fabric maker/designer and are usually discarded. However, increasingly selvedges are now being designed in such a way that they can add an interesting extra design element to your quilt.
- **Grain:** The orientation of the warp and weft threads in a woven fabric (such as quilting cotton).
- **Bias:** The grain of fabric 45 degrees to the warp and weft threads. It has the greatest stretch of any woven fabric grain.
- **Cross grain:** The grain of fabric running perpendicular to the selvedge and parallel to the weft threads.
- **Width of fabric (WOF):** The usable width between the selvedges. For quilting cotton this is typically 42in once the selvedges have been removed.

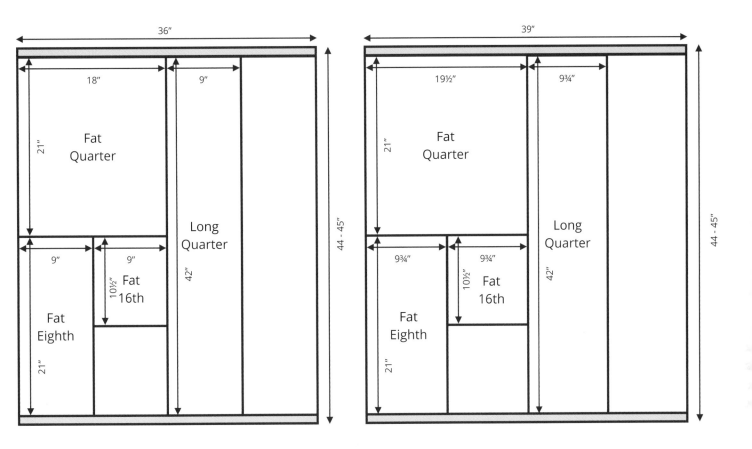

Left diagram (36" wide):

36"

18" | 9"

21"

Fat Quarter

Long Quarter

44 - 45"

42"

9" | 9"

10½"

Fat 16th

Fat Eighth

21"

Right diagram (39" wide):

39"

19½" | 9¾"

21"

Fat Quarter

Long Quarter

44 - 45"

42"

9¾" | 9¾"

10½"

Fat 16th

Fat Eighth

21"

10" x 10"

Layer Cake

5" x 5"

Charm Pack

WOF x 2½"

Jelly Roll

Quilting cotton

While quilts can be and are pieced from any fabric, a quick peek at any historic or modern quilt will confirm that cotton is the universal favourite. Cotton fabric comes in many forms depending on the intended use, so quilters tend to opt for a type called quilting cotton.

Quilting cotton is a medium-weight fabric made using 100 per cent cotton. It has a plain weave that is hard wearing and stable to sew and piece with. Generally, there is a right side and a wrong side to the fabric with the right side often being printed and the side you want to show off in your quilt, while the reverse is the side you normally want to hide inside the quilt.

Key features:
- The stability of the weave means there should be minimal shrinkage when washing.
- It presses well and can take a high heat without scorching.
- Creases set well with heat but do not come up as easily as they do in other fabrics, for example, linen.
- Cotton is a hard-wearing fabric and holds up well to intensive use and repeated washes, making it ideal for use by children and pets.
- Nowadays there is an almost limitless variety of colours and patterns available, so whatever you're looking for you are likely to be able to find.
- Depending on your needs, quilting cotton can be purchased either as yardage straight off the bolt or as pre-cuts and bundles.

TOP TIP

Make sure to write down brand and colour/print names in case you need to buy more. There's nothing more frustrating than trying to track down the right white or the exact print you need without a name.

Solids

Popular with modern quilters, solids have been a central theme in the development of the modern quilting movement. The vibrant colours and graphic feel they lend to a quilt show off modern designs brilliantly. High-quality solids are yarn dyed, which means the threads are a uniform colour throughout the weave and often have no clear right side or wrong side.

Many quilters have a preferred brand of solids that they stick to consistently, while others prefer to mix and match according to availability, the colours that they are looking for and the fabric feel. Kona Solids by Robert Kaufman and Bella Solids by Moda have the widest colour selections with over 320+ shades and hues of each and feel very similar, while Pure Solids by Art Gallery Fabrics is a thinner and finer-feeling fabric that mixes well with thin patterned fabrics. Many others are available, and it's worth experimenting to find which you prefer.

Prints

Printed quilting fabrics are no longer solely the realm of florals, pastels and woodland animals, with bold colours, whimsical prints and abstract shapes now reigning supreme. Digitally printed over a yarn-dyed solid base, the threads of printed fabric have more variation in colour when pulled apart and the right side is generally very clear (although harder to identify with white-on-white prints).

There are a wide range of manufacturers of quilting cotton and a growing number of independent small-batch printers offering a smorgasbord of choice depending on your budget and preferences. The biggest and most popular manufacturers include Moda, Makower, Andover, Riley Blake, Art Gallery Fabrics and Robert Kaufman. Many of these house designer lines and collections under their umbrella; Moda hosts Ruby Star Society, Giucy Giuce is part of Andover and Tula Pink is printed by Free Spirit Fabrics.

For those who love to bring in a little vintage feel, no discussion of quilting cotton can be complete without mention of the iconic Liberty fabrics. Much loved and highly prized by quilters for over 100 years, Liberty produces a range of very high-quality cotton fabrics in their unique historic and contemporary prints. Their Tana Lawn is a fine, cool and durable fabric with a silky feel that is best suited to delicate projects while their quilting cotton can be used in the same way as any other quilting cotton. Due to their high quality and luxury nature, Liberty fabrics are very pricy and often cost at least twice the price of most other quilting cottons.

Batting

An often overlooked but just as integral part of a quilt as quilting cotton, batting (also called wadding) is the hidden middle layer of a quilt that adds warmth, stability and determines the thickness of the finished quilt.

Made from a variety of different fibres, each brand will have a recommended maximum space between quilting lines to prevent the fibres coming apart over time when washing the quilt. The fibre type will determine the loft (also called the weight or thickness) of batting and impact the 'puffiness' of the desired finish. A high loft will be thicker and need less quilting while a low loft will be thinner and show off dense quilting better.

The most commonly available fibre options and their lofts are:

Loft	Fibre	Blend
High	Polyester	100 per cent polyester
	Wool	100 per cent wool
Low to Medium	Cotton	80 per cent cotton/20 per cent polyester
		100 per cent cotton
Low	Bamboo	50 per cent bamboo/50 per cent cotton
		100 per cent bamboo
	Silk	90 per cent silk/10 per cent polyester

Things to consider when shopping:
- Scrim is a light layer of woven fibres added to some batting to act as a stabiliser and hold the fibres together while quilting. Batting with scrim often allows for a larger spacing of your quilting lines while batting without scrim will need to be quilted more densely.
- Depending on the climate where you live, you may prefer a higher-loft thick and warm batting or a low-loft thin and light one.
- Depending on the fibre and loft of batting you opt for, the drape will have either more or less flow, with lower lofts draping more fluidly.
- Most batting is a bleached white (polyester) or natural colour (natural fibre options and blends) and are suitable for all types of projects. However, for a very dark project you may want to consider black batting.

- Pre-cut sizes can help reduce waste if you are buying for a quilt similar to one of the standard pre-cut batting sizes, while buying yardage off the bolt is a good option when you need something a little more specific and custom. Many shops only stock one type or the other so that may determine which option you go for.
- Wool is a common allergen so be mindful of your intended recipient.

THREAD

Just as a good-quality fabric will help produce a good-quality quilt, thread quality is also crucial. You should always use a good-quality thread to avoid snagging, fraying and other problems down the line. Thread types are divided broadly into two main camps: cotton and polyester. While many quilters match their thread fibre to their fabric fibre, it is important to consider the function the thread is playing in your project, and it is common to mix and match threads in a single quilt to meet specific needs.

Before you go running to your grandma's or great-aunt's sewing box to rummage among their spools of thread, remember that, unlike vintage fabrics, threads have a shelf life. They become brittle with age which leads to snapping or shredding at inopportune moments and causing tangles in your sewing machine – use with care, if at all. As with fabrics, there are a huge range of high-quality thread brands now available with two of the most popular being Aurifil for pure cotton and Wonderfil for polyester/blends.

What do all the numbers mean?

If you look closely at the bottom of a spool of thread, it will have a collection of seemingly random numbers. Each number tells a story about the spool and will help you determine if it's the right fit for your project. Not every spool will include all the shown numbers, but the majority include at least the first three.

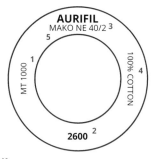

Key

1. Length
2. Colour code
3. Weight and ply
4. Fibre
5. Fibre source
6. Collection name

Length

This shows the length of thread on the spool in metres. Typically, thinner threads will fit more on a spool, for example 2000m, while thicker threads will fit less, for example 100m.

Colour code

This will look different depending on the brand, but it allows you to purchase an exact colour replica when you run out. With many thread companies offering a huge range of colours and shades it can be difficult to judge a perfect match by eye, so this code is invaluable.

Weight and ply

Sometimes just the weight of a thread is shown, and sometimes the ply is also included. Where both the weight and ply of a thread are indicated they are shown as a fraction: 40/2 means a 40-weight thread that is made of 2 plies.

WEIGHT

So, what is thread weight (wt)? The short answer is it refers to the thickness of a thread. The larger the number, the thinner the thread while the smaller the number, the thicker

the thread. The long answer is thread weight is a measurement of length calculated by determining how much a length of thread weighs:

- The easiest method of calculating is the Metric Count (NM) where length is balanced against 1kg. For example, if 40km of thread weighs 1kg, that is a 40-weight thread. Likewise, if 12km weighs 1kg, that is a 12wt thread, 80km is an 80wt thread and so on.
- Another method is the English Count (NE) where a 1lb weight is balanced against hanks of thread each 840 yards long. For example, if 28 hanks weigh 1lb it is a 28wt thread, 50 hanks equal a 50wt thread and so on.

The Metric Count is commonly used for synthetic threads while the English Count is typically used for cotton threads. Some brands include the weight calculation method in their labelling, for example Aurifil uses the English Count system as shown by the NE before 40/2.

PLY

The thread ply number shows the number of plies (also known as strands) which have been twisted together. For example, a 2-ply thread has two strands twisted together to form the thread, a 3-ply has three strands twisted together, and so on. Generally, the more plies a thread has the stronger it is.

Fibre

This shows if the thread is made of pure cotton, polyester or a blend.

Fibre source

Natural fibre threads occasionally indicate the source of the cotton used. Aurifil uses 100 per cent Egyptian cotton grown in the Mako region of Egypt on the river Nile, as shown by the inclusion of 'MAKO' on the spool label.

Product line

This identifies which thread collection or product line a specific spool is from when a manufacturer has a large range with otherwise similar number indicators. The Decobob indicator on a Wonderfil spool shows that it is a cottonised polyester thread with a textured matte finish, treated in such a way that it behaves more like cotton.

Choosing your thread

Before reaching for the nearest thread to hand, pause and consider what you need the thread to achieve: are you piecing blocks, and if so, by hand or machine? Are you quilting, and again by machine or hand? What role do you want the quilting thread to play in the overall design and visual impact of your quilt?

As you can see in the table, the thicker a thread is the better suited it is for hand quilting while the thinner it is, the better it is for delicate paper piecing and stitching seams by hand. Most quilters keep 50wt threads to hand due to their versatility, closely followed by 40wt.

Type	Weights	Suitable for
Heavy weight	8wt	Hand quilting
	12wt	Hand quilting
		Machine quilting
	28wt	Machine quilting
Medium weight	40wt	Machine piecing
		Machine quilting
	50wt	Machine piecing
		Foundation Paper Piecing
		English Paper Piecing
		Hand piecing
		Machine quilting
Light weight	80wt and above	Foundation Paper Piecing
		English Paper Piecing
		Hand piecing

NEEDLES

When it comes to sewing, needles are not just a tool but an extension of your hand – they are how you make stitches and should be carefully considered and chosen for each stage of a project, the thread you're using and the finish you wish to achieve.

A general rule of thumb is to change your needle every six to ten hours of sewing time or every one or two quilts, depending on how large and intensive the stitching on each quilt is. Neither of those gauges is very precise and rely on you paying close attention to how long you've been stitching for, so instead here are some signs that it's time to change your needle:

- Thread starts regularly breaking or shredding when it normally sews without issues.
- Your sewing machine starts to skip stitches.
- Fabrics are puckering, getting marked or becoming damaged.
- It is getting harder to push the needle through your fabric.
- The plating on a hand-sewing needle is wearing off.

Machine needles

Unlike thread-weight numbering, machine needles are numbered in a much more straightforward way. They are formed of two numbers, the larger of which indicates the European needle size with the smaller indicating the American size. The European scale ranges from 60 to 120 while the American scale is from 8 to 20. Needle sizes are shown as 80/12, 90/14 and so on. The larger the needle number, the thicker the fabric you can sew through.

Machine needles come in many different types suited to a wide range of fabrics, but as a quilter the two you will be relying on are universal and quilting needles. Universal needles have slightly rounded tips and are well suited to sewing stable, woven fabric such as quilting cotton. Quilting needles are specially strengthened to enable them to pierce multiple layers of fabric and batting cleanly.

So which needle should you use and when? When doing standard piecing using quilting cotton, a universal 80/12 needle is ideal, while when quilting a basted quilt sandwich a quilting 90/14 needle should always be used. The thickness of thread being used will also impact needle choice as while the eye of an 80/12 can easily accommodate 40wt, 50wt and 80wt threads, 12wt and 28wt threads cannot run smoothly through and are likely to snag and snap frequently and are therefore better suited to a 90/14 needle size.

Hand-sewing needles

In contrast to machine needles, hand-sewing needles are numbered in a comparable way to thread weights where the smaller the number, the thicker the needle is and the higher the number, the finer the needle is.

Fabric/thread type	Needle size
Heavy weight	2
	3
	4
Medium weight	5
	6
	7
	8
	9
	10
Light weight	11
	12

Needle types include:

- **Sharps:** these are short to medium in length and are a good all-purpose needle suited to a wide range of hand sewing.
- **Embroidery/Crewel:** these have a slightly elongated eye to allow for multiple strands of thread or thicker threads to pass through easily and are well suited to big stitch hand quilting.
- **Quilting/Betweens:** these are short needles designed to allow small and precise stitches when hand quilting with light or medium weight thread.
- **Milliners'/Straw:** these have a longer needle length and are popular with many English Paper Piecing enthusiasts.

ADAPTING FOR ACCESSIBILITY

The sewing and quilting industry is generally lagging in terms of accessibility to help everyone be able to participate regardless of their individual needs, but thankfully there is some movement in the right direction with some brands starting to release more accessible tools. Prym is doing particularly well on this front and has one of the wider selections of tools available.

Below are some general hints and tips that you may find helpful, but please remember this is not intended to be an exhaustive list and instead should be used as a starting point for exploring some options that could be helpful.

Accessible sewing tools

- Easy-grip pins with larger ergonomic heads can be very helpful for those with low dexterity or a low grip in their hands. If pins are still a struggle, often they can be swapped out for binding clips which may be easier to handle.
- Needle threaders come in many different styles and are great for anyone who struggles with the dexterity, eyesight or patience required to thread a needle.
- Quilting ruler handles can make holding a ruler in place while cutting fabric or trimming blocks easier for anyone wanting to reduce hand and wrist strain or who has a low grip.
- Silicon iron rests reduce the need to frequently lift a heavy iron up and down and at difficult angles, helping reduce strain on wrists and arm joints.
- Seam rippers with ergonomic handles are easier to use for those with low dexterity or grip.
- Easy-grip scissors are squeezed to cut fabric unlike the wider motion needed by traditional scissors and can be helpful to anyone with a low grip.
- Anti-fatigue mats can help reduce pressure on ankles, knees and hips when standing, for example when pressing or cutting fabric.
- Mid- and high-end sewing machines now often come with a variety of accessibility friendly features, from automatic needle threaders and thread cutters to pedal-free sewing and knee lifts and more, and are worth investigating (within the bounds of any budgetary restraints).

Tips for reducing strain when sewing

- Batching and breaking down tasks can be a great way of making the most of times when you feel energised, to set yourself up for an easier time when you're less energised but still want to sew. For example, if cutting fabric for a project tends to drain you, try cutting out bits of a project each time you're feeling up to it so that you eventually have the whole project cut without the strain of cutting it all at once. Similarly, if you find binding easy, consider letting a few quilts pile up ready for binding when you need a low-energy sewing session.

- Sitting to cut and iron where possible rather than standing can significantly reduce the fatigue and strain of standing for extended periods of time.

- If you find your energy crashing after every sewing session, try setting a timer for the maximum period you feel you can sew for without overextending yourself. Remember that you can always stop at any time before the alarm, but it can be good to have a reminder that it is time to take a break.

- If you struggle more at certain times of day, try carving out time when you're feeling more energised. For example, if evenings find you slowing down but you're a morning person, try some early-morning sewing to start your day.

- Remember that quilting is very physical, so it is important to stay hydrated and take regular breaks. Some light stretching before and after a sewing session can reduce soreness, especially in the shoulders.

CHAPTER 4

GETTING STARTED

N ow you have the equipment and materials you need to start making your first quilt, it's finally time to start sewing.

This chapter will walk you through all the key skills you need to start piecing your own blocks and is packed with all the tips and tricks you need to make transforming fabric into a quilt top less intimidating. From safely using a rotary cutter to cutting fabric to sewing and pressing accurate seams and perfectly trimming your blocks, this chapter helps you learn to do it all.

USING A ROTARY CUTTER

When it comes to cutting fabric, trimming blocks and squaring up quilts, a rotary cutter is the quilter's best friend and will be an indispensable tool throughout your quilting journey. Safety is paramount when using a rotary cutter – you are wielding a sharp blade that can cause considerable damage if misused. To make sure you stay safe, simply follow these basic rules of rotary cutter safety (plus a dash of common sense):

- If it isn't in your hand, the blade should be covered.
- Always cut away from or across your body, never towards yourself. When cutting across your body always cut from your dominant side: if you are right-handed cut from right to left and vice versa.
- Don't walk around with an open blade.
- Never touch the edge of the blade – it is very sharp and can easily injure you if mishandled.

STEP-BY-STEP: USING A ROTARY CUTTER

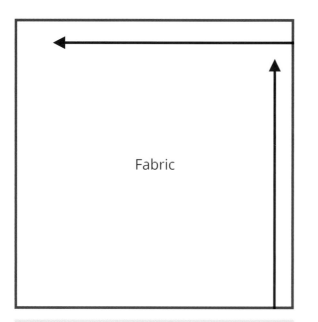

Fabric

Your body

Basic usage

Whichever style of rotary cutter you have (*see* Chapter 3 for discussion of different types), the process for using it in conjunction with a quilting ruler is always the same.

Step 1: Align the quilting ruler so that the ruler covers the fabric you want to keep. This prevents you having to keep squaring up repeatedly if you are a little wobbly and reduces fabric waste from having to keep retrimming.

Step 2: Spread the fingers on your non-dominant hand out and apply firm pressure to hold the quilting ruler in place without it slipping on the fabric.

Step 3: Align the side of your rotary cutter with the edge of the quilting ruler so that they are touching.

Step 4: Applying even pressure, move the rotary cutter along the edge of the quilting ruler until you have cut the desired distance.

TOP TIPS

- If you keep missing the threads at the beginning of a cut, try doing a little run-up to the start of the fabric to help catch the beginning edge.
- Keep an even pressure along the whole cutting distance – variations can cause the blade to skip sections or not fully cut through your fabric.
- Check you have fully cut the fabric before moving your ruler by gently nudging the uncovered fabric out of the way, being careful not to pull it out from under the ruler if it hasn't been properly cut.
- If you find you regularly have small threads that haven't been cut despite using an even pressure, it may be time to change your rotary cutter blade for a fresh one.
- If you struggle to keep the ruler in place while cutting a longer length (for example 24in), try gently moving your hand along the ruler in a crab-like motion as you cut or using your forearm to hold the ruler in place.

CUTTING FABRIC

From straightening the edge of a fat quarter to cutting pieces for sewing blocks, you will almost always need to cut your fabric before you start sewing.

Squaring fabric

When cutting fabric, it is important to square the edge. This means cutting a straight edge on your fabric to use when aligning rulers for cutting strips or pieces to help you make the most of your fabric. The most common times when you will need to square fabric is when cutting from a fat quarter or from yardage – both methods are covered here and can also be applied to any other shape or size of fabric you may have.

Remember to trim the selvedge off your fabric before cutting pieces you wish to sew with, to prevent it showing in your finished quilt – unless, of course, you want it to!

TOP TIP

If you need to make a large cut that is bigger than one ruler you can either use removable tape to hold two rulers together to give the required length, or purchase ruler connectors that do the same job.

STEP-BY-STEP: CUTTING FAT QUARTERS (FQS)

Depending on where you bought your FQs, the shop may have squared the edges already for you. However, it is likely that you will encounter an un-squared FQ often in your quilting journey.

Step 1: Using a quilting ruler longer than the edge you wish to trim (a 6½ × 24in quilting ruler is typically the best suited), line it up along an edge so that it covers the edge of the fabric you wish to keep and leaves just a sliver of fabric to be discarded.

Step 2: Applying even pressure, move the rotary cutter along the edge of the quilting ruler to cut the small amount of excess and discard.

Step 3: All future fabric cuts should be aligned against this trimmed edge so that you have neat 90-degree square edges.

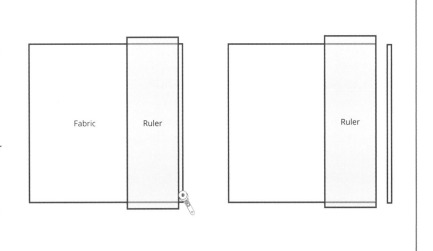

Many quilt patterns will need more than a fat quarter of fabric and so give requirements in yardage. Although quilting cotton yardage is usually 42–44in from selvedge to selvedge, it is typically sold and cut folded in half. This means that the cutting edge is only 21in–22in, making it possible to cut long strips without having to move your ruler along as you go.

Step 1: Using a 6½ × 24in quilting ruler, align the long side along the edge so that it covers the edge of the fabric you wish to keep and leaves just a sliver of fabric to be discarded, and line up the horizontal ruler lines with the fold. These edges should be at right angles to ensure longer strips do not have a bend when unfolded.

Step 2: Applying even pressure, move the rotary cutter along the edge of the quilting ruler to cut the small amount of excess and discard it.

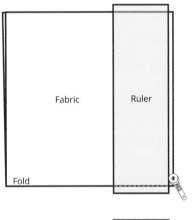

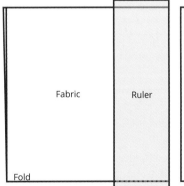

Step 3: All future fabric cuts can be aligned with this trimmed edge and the folded edge so that you have neat and square edges.

TOP TIP

Place the fold towards you to help keep the fabric truly square when squaring the edge or when cutting long strips that will be unfolded.

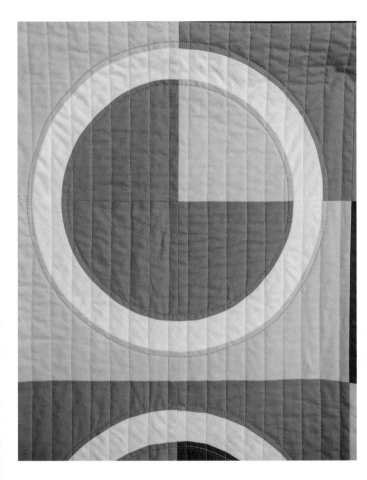

Cutting pieces

Cutting fabric into small pieces ready for sewing back together again is at the very core of quilting – how else could quilters create the detailed blocks and quilts they're so well known for? Whether cutting individual pieces or sub-cutting from a larger strip, accuracy is especially important at this stage – errors can have potentially large knock-on effects later down the line.

STEP-BY-STEP: CUTTING INDIVIDUAL PIECES

When making just one block or when using lots of different fabrics, for example in a scrappy quilt, you often need just one or two pieces in a given size. Rather than cutting a whole strip to sub-cut, it is more economical to simply cut what you need from a corner of the fabric instead.

Step 1: Starting with a squared edge of fabric, square the adjoining edge so that you have a 90-degree corner.

Step 2: Align the appropriate lines on your ruler with the squared corner. For example, if you want to cut a piece of fabric 4in wide and 6in tall, align the vertical 4in line with the vertical squared edge and the horizontal 6in line with the horizontal squared edge.

Step 3: Cut up and across the edge of the ruler.

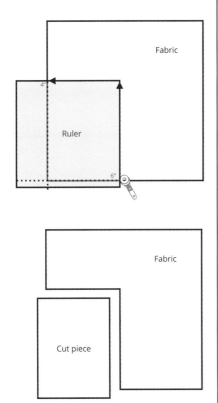

STEP-BY-STEP: STRIP CUTTING

If you need a lot of one-size squares or rectangles, cutting strips and then sub-cutting them into the required size is both faster than cutting each piece individually and reduces the chance of cutting errors.

Step 1: Starting with a squared edge of fabric, align the appropriate line of your ruler with the fabric edge at the required strip width.

Step 2: Cut a strip the length of your fabric.

Step 3: Rotating the cut strip 90 degrees, square off the left side if not already square. Working from left to right (if you are left-handed square the right side and work from right to left), cut the required width of pieces from the strip until you have the number needed. For example, if you have cut your strip at 3in wide and want pieces 3 × 2in, cut at 2in intervals.

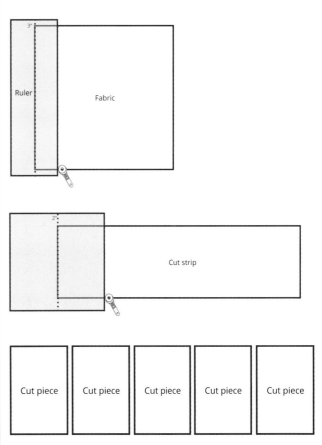

SEWING ACCURATE SEAMS

Quilting seams are universally set at ¼in wide as a standard, meaning that the stitching line is ¼in away from the edge of the fabric. As with every universal rule, there are of course some exceptions to this; for example, the seams on a quilt back are often ½in and a pattern may occasionally specify another seam width such as a scant quarter (slightly smaller than a standard ¼in).

As with cutting pieces of fabric for piecing, sewing seams as accurately as possible is an important skill to practise. Sewing a seam at ⅜in rather than the instructed ¼in may not seem like the end of the world, but when added up across several blocks it will result in a smaller finished block than anticipated. This might not be a huge issue for some projects, but for others it can severely impact the finished look.

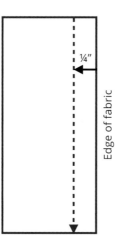

¼"

Edge of fabric

TOP TIP

If you find that you often get a tangle of threads at the beginning of a seam, try using a leader to help give you a smoother start. A leader is a small scrap of fabric placed under the needle at the beginning of sewing to prevent these tangles and ensure a smooth start to your seam when stitching blocks together. Simply cut the joining threads afterwards and keep the leader ready to reuse.

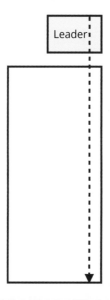

Leader

STEP-BY-STEP: SEWING STANDARD SEAMS

A ¼in quilter's foot is a very helpful tool for helping you sew accurate seams and is highly recommended as a first purchase when expanding your quilting toolkit beyond the essentials. If you don't have a ¼in foot, check the markings on your stitching plate as this should show a ¼in line for you to use as a guide. Alternatively, you can use a ruler and some washi/removable tape to mark a line ¼in from the needle stitching line.

Step 1: Place your fabric right sides together along the sides you wish to join.

Step 2: Optional: pin your fabric together using straight pins or binding clips to hold in place.

Step 3: Aligning the edges of your fabric with the edge of your ¼in foot or ¼in guide, sew a straight line along the entire length of your seam. Take care to remove any pins and clips before sewing over them to prevent injury from broken needles or pins.

Step 4: Cut your threads and press as required.

STEP-BY-STEP: SEWING SCANT QUARTER SEAMS

A scant quarter is a seam sewn one to two thread widths smaller than a standard ¼in. This helps give greater accuracy when piecing very precise shapes or points as it eliminates the slight bulk your thread adds to a standard seam.

Step 1: Move your needle position one or two positions to the right/closer to your ¼in foot or guide.

Step 2: Sew the seam as if it was a standard ¼in seam.

Unpicking seams

While it can be frustrating, slip-ups happen. Don't feel bad if you find yourself reaching for the seam ripper – you are only human, and mistakes happen to everyone. Before unpicking the offending seam, ask yourself if you really need to unpick it. Is it going to affect the quilt pattern, for example, has the block been sewn upside down? Is it a mistake that only you see? If only you are going to notice it, is it going to annoy you if you don't fix it, or can you live with it? If the answer is yes, it needs to be unpicked, there are two methods for ripping out your stitches.

STEP-BY-STEP: TWO WAYS TO UNPICK SEAMS

Method 1

Step 1: Pulling the seam apart to show the stitches holding it together, insert the sharp point of the seam ripper and carefully cut a few stitches.

Step 2: Turning so that the protective ball is facing down, carefully slide the blade along the seam to cut all the required stitches.

Step 3: Use a lint brush to gently remove the cut thread ends.

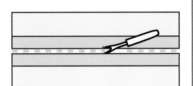

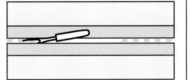

Method 2

Step 1: Lay the seam flat with fabrics right sides together. Use the sharp point of the seam ripper to carefully cut stitches every three to four stitches along the length you need to unpick.

Step 2: Turn the seam over and carefully pull the now loose back thread away from the fabric.

Step 3: Remove cut thread ends using a lint brush.

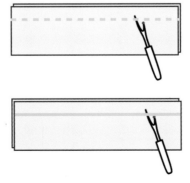

Chain and web piecing

When doing a lot of piecing for a quilt, batch piecing can be a great way to speed up the process as well as reduce thread wastage by cutting down on the thread tails needed for each piece. There are two main methods of batch piecing: chain piecing and web piecing. Chain piecing is the process of sewing prepared pieces of fabric continuously without stopping to cut your threads between sections, while web piecing is the method of chain piecing multiple blocks into rows/columns without cutting threads between joined sections.

TOP TIP

Keep an eye on your bobbin thread so that it doesn't run out while you keep 'sewing' only to have to re-sew your blocks.

STEP-BY-STEP: HOW TO CHAIN PIECE

Chain piecing can be used for virtually every quilt pattern you want to make, even Foundation Paper Piecing. It saves time, cuts down on thread waste and helps you to keep track of what you're sewing when assembling lots of blocks at once.

Step 1: Cut all the fabric for the blocks you need to sew.

Step 2: Align the first two pieces right sides together so that they are ready to sew.

Step 3: Lay them out next to your sewing machine in the order you want to sew, or stack them if you prefer. This helps keep everything in order and stops you accidentally sewing the wrong pieces together.

Step 4: Sew the first pair as you normally would, but instead of cutting the threads at the end, gently feed the next pair under the foot. The feed dogs will 'grab' it and pull it forward to sew as normal.

Step 5: Repeat until all your pairs are sewn and cut the joining threads.

Web piecing takes chain piecing to the next level – instead of cutting your chain-pieced blocks apart after piecing, if you piece them in order, you can then join them to form a larger web. This method is ideal for piecing larger blocks where the orientation of each sub-block is important as it helps keep everything neatly in its place.

Step 1: Chain piece your blocks or cut fabric together in loose columns. Press the seams as desired but do not cut threads to separate the blocks.

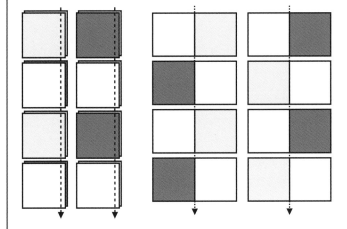

Step 2: Sew the loose columns together in rows so that all the seams along the row are joined. Press seams as desired.

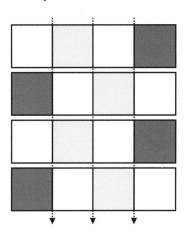

Step 3: Join the rows together to form the assembled block/quilt. Press seams – if you are pressing your seams open you will need to cut the initial joining threads at this point.

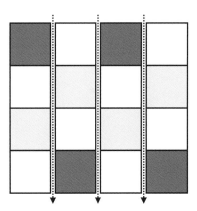

PRESSING SEAMS

Pressing is the process of setting the fabric of your seam allowance either to one side or open to help merge your stitches into the fabric and create permanent folds in the fabric along the seam line. Pressing gives you flatter seams, resulting in less overall bulk in your quilt as well as making it easier to match seams while piecing. There are no hard and fast rules when it comes to which way you should press your seams: some patterns will give instructions to help reduce seam bulk or make nesting seams easier, while others will leave it up to your discretion.

Most pressing should be done with an iron as the heat helps set the seam effectively, but you can also finger press or use a seam roller for temporary pressing:

- Finger pressing is where you use the heat from your fingers or the back of a nail edge to press a seam or fold into fabric instead of an iron. Often used to mark the middle of a block or piece of fabric.
- A seam roller is a tool used to manually press seams without the need for a hot iron. This is especially useful in Foundation Paper Piecing.

Sewing with white fabric gives rise to its own specific problems when pressing as it shows darker fabric and threads quite easily which can affect the finished look of your quilt. If you can, it is recommended to press seams involving white fabric open but if this is not possible (for example you need to nest your seams), you should trim any loose threads along the seams to stop darker threads showing through the white fabric when quilted.

Pressing to the side

POSITIVES:
- Quick and easy to do.
- Helps nest seams.
- Avoids fabric shadowing if pressing to the dark side.

NEGATIVES:
- If seams aren't alternated, joins can become bulky where seams are pressed in the same direction.

Pressing open

POSITIVES:
- Reduces bulk at seam junctions when quilting.
- Darker fabrics won't show through lighter ones as they are pressed against themselves.

NEGATIVES:
- Can be fiddlier than pressing to the side with a risk of burning your fingers.

MATCHING SEAMS

When joining blocks together, matching your seams ensures that block corners meet in neat squares, that points are sharp and precise, and that the construction lines are smooth and continuous to avoid distracting the eye from the overall design and fabric placement. There are two main methods for seam matching depending on how the seams were pressed: nested to the side and open.

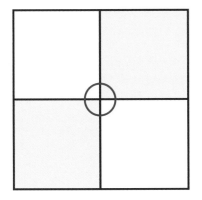

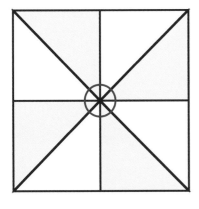

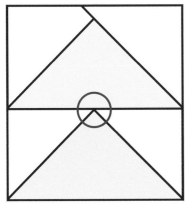

- To perfectly match points, flip the seam over so that the side with the point is facing upwards and then sew the seam line exactly over the tip of the point.
- Accurate block trimming will do much of the work for you when matching seams and points.
- If the gap between seam matches is longer than approximately 6in, pop a straight pin parallel to the seam around ½in from the edge of the fabric to help keep everything in place, preventing slippage and bunching or puckering.

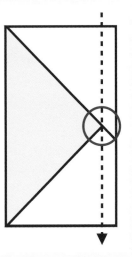

STEP-BY-STEP: NESTED SEAMS

The easiest way of matching seams is to nest them by pressing adjoining seams to the side in opposite directions so that they fit snugly together when sewn and give you crisp corners and points.

Step 1: Join all the blocks in the first row of your block or quilt top and press seams to the right.

Step 2: Join all the blocks in the second row and press seams to the left.

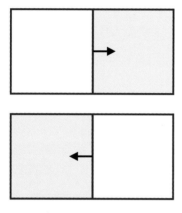

Step 3: Repeat until all rows are joined and pressed, alternating the pressing direction for each row.

Step 4: Join the pressed rows in order. The seams will fit nicely next to each other helping you to make sure each row matches the next neatly.

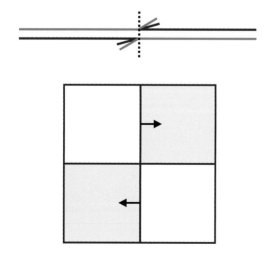

STEP-BY-STEP: OPEN SEAMS

Matching open seams gives a flatter finish than nested seams and although they do take a little more time and care to match perfectly, the precise finish is often worth the extra effort.

Step 1: With right sides together, place a straight pin vertically on either side of the seam or point you want to match, ensuring that the seam lines are exactly aligned.

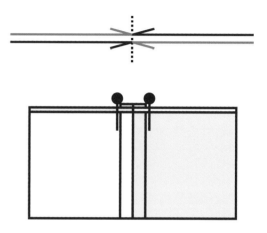

Step 2: Sew along the seam, making sure to remove pins as you come to them and going slowly over the matched section. If you feel the fabric shifting, use the end of a pin or stiletto point to hold it in position once the adjoining pins have been removed.

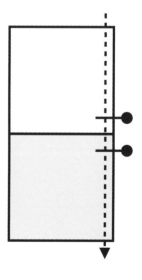

TRIMMING BLOCKS

Many block instructions produce slightly oversize blocks to allow for trimming down. Accurate trimming will help you to match your seams more precisely and keep everything at the required sizes for assembly so it's worth taking your time with this stage. Remember that blocks are trimmed to ½in larger than they will finish to allow for ¼in seam allowances on all sides, so do not be alarmed that the block initially seems to be bigger than your desired finished size.

TOP TIPS

- Iron press seams for a block before trimming.
- Use removeable tape on your ruler to make the lines clearer when trimming lots of the same block.

STEP-BY-STEP: HALF-SQUARE TRIANGLE (HST)

Step 1: Align the 45-degree line on your quilting ruler with the diagonal seam on the HST, checking that the HST fits within the required trimming size. For example, if you want your trimmed block to be 3½ × 3½in, align the intersection of the 3½in lines with the diagonal seam line.

Step 3: Rotate the HST 180 degrees. Align the diagonal seam with the 45-degree ruler line and the intersection of the required trimming size with the trimmed corner of the block.

Step 4: Cut up and across the edge of the ruler, discarding trimmings.

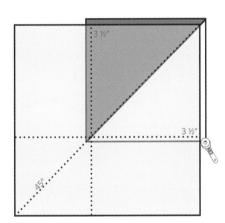

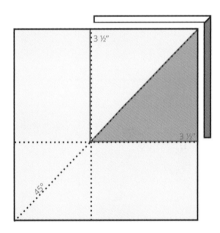

Step 2: Cut up and across the edge of the ruler, discarding trimmings.

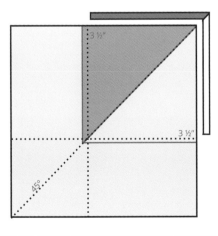

STEP-BY-STEP: QUARTER-SQUARE TRIANGLE (QST)

Step 1: Align the 45-degree line on your quilting ruler with the diagonal seam on the QST, checking that the block fits within the required trimming size and centring the middle of the block at half of the finished trim size. For example, if you want your trimmed block to be 4½ × 4½in, align the intersection of the 4½in ruler lines with the diagonal seam line and the centre of the block with the intersection of the 2¼in ruler lines.

Step 2: Cut up and across the edge of the ruler, discarding trimmings.

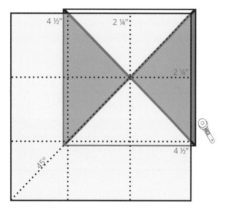

Step 3: Rotate the QST 180 degrees. Align the diagonal seam with the 45-degree ruler line and the intersection of the required trimming size with the trimmed corner of the block.

Step 4: Cut up and across the edge of the ruler, discarding trimmings.

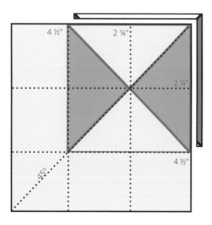

STEP-BY-STEP: FLYING GEESE

Step 1: Align the point of the Flying Geese triangle at the intersection of half the finished trim size and ¼in on your quilting ruler. For example, if you want your trimmed block to be 4½ × 2½in, align the tip of the triangle with the intersection of the ¼in and 2¼in ruler lines.

Step 2: Align the bottom right corner of the triangle with the ruler line corresponding to the trimmed block height. For example, for a 2½in tall block, align the triangle corner with the 2½in ruler line.

Step 3: Check that the block fits within the desired trim size, then cut up and across the edge of the ruler, discarding trimmings.

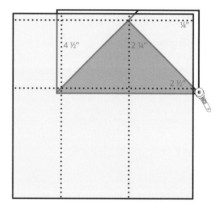

Step 4: Rotate the block 180 degrees. Align the intersection of the required trimming size with the trimmed corner of the block, ensuring that the bottom points of the triangle are ¼in in from the bottom and sides of the block trim size.

Step 5: Cut up and across the edge of the ruler, discarding trimmings.

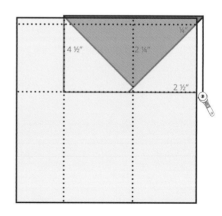

STEP-BY-STEP: HALF-RECTANGLE TRIANGLE (HRT)

Step 1: Align the diagonal seam with the intersection of the ¼in ruler lines at each end. For example, if you want your trimmed HRT to be 4½ × 2 ½in, align the top of the diagonal seam with the intersection of the ¼in ruler lines and the bottom of the seam with the 4¼in and 2¼in ruler lines.

Note: The seam line will not go exactly into the corner of the block as it is not a 45-degree angle and should instead be just to the side of the corner.

Step 2: Cut up and across the edge of the ruler, discarding trimmings.

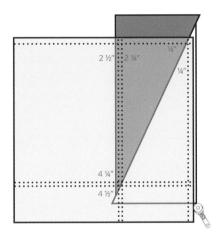

Step 3: Rotate the HRT 180 degrees. Align the intersection of the required trimming size with the trimmed corner of the block.

Step 4: Cut up and across the edge of the ruler, discarding trimmings.

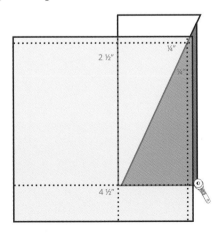

STEP-BY-STEP: SQUARE-IN-A-SQUARE (SIAS)

Step 1: Align the top and right points of the central square at the intersection of half the finished trim size and ¼in on your quilting ruler. For example, if you want your trimmed block to be 4½ × 4½in, align the points of the square with the intersection of the ¼in and 2¼in ruler lines.

Step 2: Check that the block fits within the desired trim size, then cut up and across the edge of the ruler, discarding trimmings.

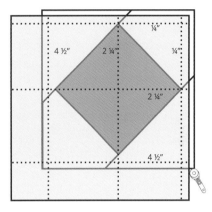

Step 3: Rotate the block 180 degrees. Align the intersection of the required trimming size with the trimmed corner of the block, ensuring that the bottom and left points of the square are ¼in in from the bottom and sides of the block trim size.

Step 4: Cut up and across the edge of the ruler, discarding trimmings.

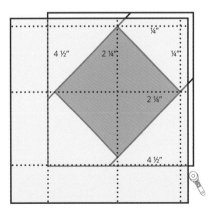

STEP-BY-STEP: QUARTER CIRCLE

Step 1: Align the curved seam with the intersection of the ¼in ruler lines with the required position at each end. For example, if you want your trimmed Quarter Circle to be 4½ × 4½in with the circle position 1in from the edge of the trimmed block, align the top of the curved seam with the intersection of the ¼in and 1in ruler lines and the bottom of the seam with the 4¼in and 3½in ruler lines.

Step 2: Cut up and across the edge of the ruler, discarding trimmings.

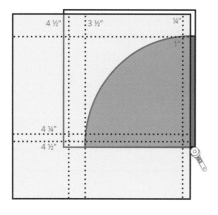

Step 3: Rotate the block 180 degrees. Align the intersection of the required trimming size with the trimmed corner of the block.

Step 4: Cut up and across the edge of the ruler, discarding trimmings.

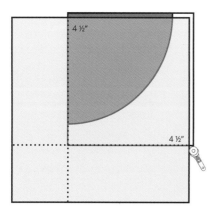

STEP-BY-STEP: ORANGE PEEL

Step 1: Align the points of the curves with the intersection of the ruler lines ¼in in from the trimming size at each end. For example, if you want your trimmed Orange Peel to be 4½ × 4½in, align the top of the curved seam with the intersection of the ¼in ruler lines and the bottom of the seam with the 4¼in ruler lines.

Step 2: Cut up and across the edge of the ruler, discarding trimmings.

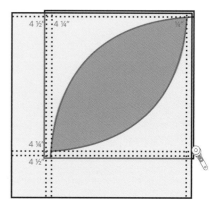

Step 3: Rotate the block 180 degrees. Align the intersection of the required trimming size with the trimmed corner of the block.

Step 4: Cut up and across the edge of the ruler, discarding trimmings.

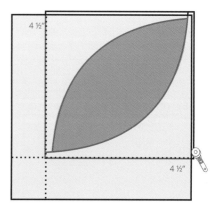

CHAPTER 5

BLOCKS AND TECHNIQUES

There are as many quilt blocks as there are quilters in the world, but most quilts are based on a core set of standard blocks and techniques.

Quilt blocks are quite literally the building blocks of a pieced quilt and can refer to the smallest sub sections, as well as larger sections made from smaller sub-blocks, depending on what the pattern calls for. For larger blocks with multiple stages of construction, the smallest pieced building blocks are sometimes called sub-blocks. A quilt technique is simply that – a method of piecing your fabric in a specific way to create a particular shape or effect.

This chapter will walk you through step-by-step instructions for the 26 core blocks and techniques you need to start making your own quilts with confidence. Each of the quilt projects in Chapter 7 uses a selection of the techniques covered here so you'll be whipping up quilts in no time. And remember – there are no quilt police so don't worry if your first, second or even twentieth tries aren't quite perfect: they're perfectly imperfect and all that matters is that you enjoy making them.

To make any of these blocks in other sizes, see the block tables for all the formulae you need to make your desired size.

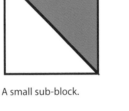

A small sub-block.

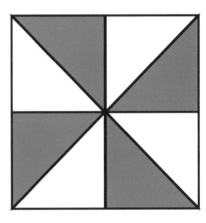

A large block made of smaller sub-blocks.

Fabrics used in sample: Bella Solids White Bleached (A), Kona Turquoise (B), Kona Pacific (C), Kona Nightfall (D), Kona Sunny (E)

KEY

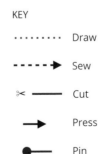

· · · · · · · · · Draw

- - - - ▶ Sew

✂ —— Cut

——▶ Press

●—— Pin

TOP TIP

If you make the 20 starred blocks in this chapter, you've almost made the Modern Sampler quilt in Chapter 7 – just add sashing! Fabric requirements and cutting instructions for each individual block are given below; for full sampler instructions, *see* Chapter 7.

STRIP PIECING*

Strip Piecing is the process of joining long strips of fabric together into one large unit before cutting into smaller individual blocks/shapes. When making lots of the same striped block, this technique saves you a lot of time and ensures greater accuracy over many identical blocks.

STEP-BY-STEP: HOW TO STRIP PIECE

Step 1: Take your 2 × 20in strips and piece in order (fabric B then fabric C then fabric D) along the long edge, pressing seams open.

Step 2: Cut your pieced panels into three 6½ ×x 6½in Strip Pieced blocks.

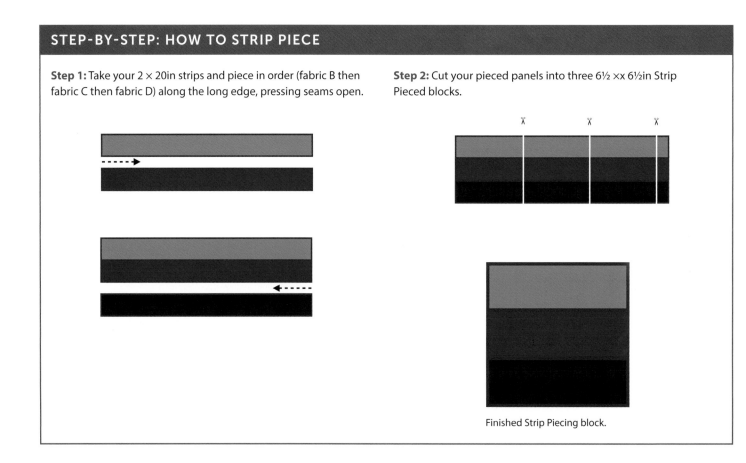

Finished Strip Piecing block.

FOUR-PATCH*

Four-Patch blocks are, as the name suggests, blocks made up of four patches. These patches can be pieced in their own respect, but you're going to start with simple squares to make a fun chequerboard block.

YOU WILL NEED

- Two 3½ × 3½in squares (fabric C)
- Two 3½ × 3½in squares (fabric E)

Finished size: 6 × 6in
Unfinished size: 6½ × 6½in
Makes one block

TOP TIP

Pay careful attention to the rotation of your sub-blocks when joining your final seam to avoid unpicking.

STEP-BY-STEP: HOW TO MAKE A FOUR-PATCH

Step 1: Sew a square of fabric C together with a square of fabric E as shown, pressing seams towards fabric C.

Step 2: Repeat so that you have two joined sub-blocks.

Step 3: Join the two sub-blocks along the long edge as shown, nesting the pressed seams to give you a neat join. Press the final seam open.

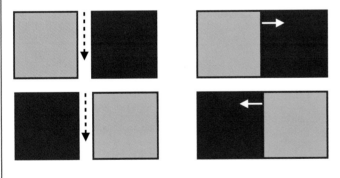 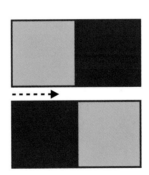 

Finished Four-Patch block.

NINE-PATCH*

As with Four-Patch blocks, Nine-Patch blocks are made of nine patches in three rows of three. These blocks are extremely common and often involve pieced squares forming seemingly complicated but easy-to-make blocks. Don't panic though – you're going to start with simple squares.

YOU WILL NEED

- Four 2½ × 2½in squares (fabric B)
- Four 2½ × 2½in squares (fabric E)
- One 2½ × 2½in square (fabric C)

Finished size: 6 × 6in
Unfinished size: 6½ × 6½in
Makes one block

TOP TIP

Pay careful attention to the rotation of your sub-blocks when joining your final seams to avoid unpicking.

STEP-BY-STEP: HOW TO MAKE A NINE-PATCH

Step 1: Sew a square of fabric B together with a square of fabric E and then another square of fabric B as shown.

Step 2: Repeat to form rows 2 and 3 using fabrics B, C and E as shown, being careful to press your seams in the direction of the arrows.

Step 3: Join the rows along the long edges, nesting the pressed seams to give you a neat join. Press the final seams open.

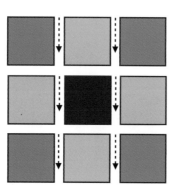

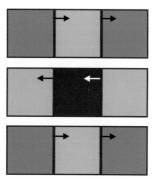

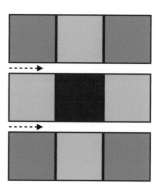

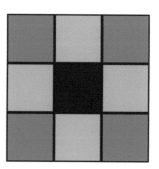

Finished Nine-Patch block.

DISAPPEARING NINE-PATCH*

Disappearing Nine-Patch (D9P) blocks are a little bit magical. They're an easy way to make an almost endless variety of seemingly complicated blocks, without the hassle of piecing each of those small patches individually. This 'slice and stitch' technique doesn't have to be restricted to nine-patches – you can do this to any block you feel brave enough to chop up to create some amazing effects.

YOU WILL NEED

- Two 2¾ × 2¾in squares (fabric A)
- Four 2¾ × 2¾in squares (fabric B)
- Two 2¾ × 2¾in squares (fabric D)
- One 2¾ × 2¾in square (fabric E)

Finished size: 6 × 6in
Unfinished size: 6½ × 6½in
Makes one block

TOP TIP

Play around with the rotation of your cut Nine-Patch squares before re-joining to find your favourite arrangement.

STEP-BY-STEP: HOW TO MAKE A DISAPPEARING NINE-PATCH

Step 1: Sew a Nine-Patch block as shown.

Step 2: Carefully cut your assembled Nine-Patch block into four 3½ × 3½in squares.

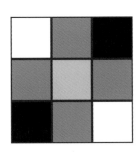
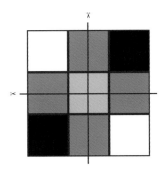

Step 3: Rotate your four cut squares as shown and join following the same process as a standard Four-Patch block.

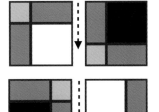
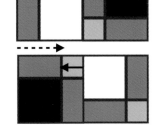

Step 4: Press the joining seam open and trim the block down to 6½ × 6½in square.

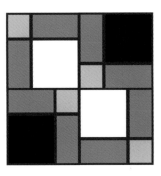

Finished Disappearing Nine-Patch block.

SNOWBALL CORNERS*

Sometimes called the 'stitch and flip' method, Snowball Corners are great for adding small triangles to shapes without adding multiple seams by fully inserting them into the construction of your block.

YOU WILL NEED

- Four 2½ × 2½in squares (fabric E)
- One 6½ × 6½in square (fabric C)

Finished size: 6 × 6in
Unfinished size: 6½ × 6½in
Makes one block

TOP TIP

If making larger blocks and your corner squares are big enough, sew another line ½in away from the main stitching line so that when you trim the corner off, you have ready-made Half-Square Triangles to use in another project.

STEP-BY-STEP: HOW TO MAKE SNOWBALL CORNERS

Step 1: Place a square of fabric E right sides together on one corner of the fabric C square and mark a diagonal line from corner to corner on the fabric E square using tailor's chalk or a removable fabric pen as shown.

Step 2: Backstitching two to four stitches at the beginning and end of each sew line, sew along the marked line and trim excess to ¼in seam allowance. Flip back the corner and press the seam open.

Step 3: Repeat with remaining three corners.

Finished Snowball Corners block.

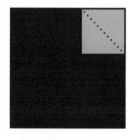
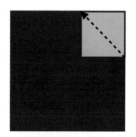
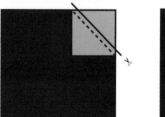

HALF-SQUARE TRIANGLES

Arguably the most versatile quilt block, Half-Square Triangles (or HSTs as they are commonly known) are two right-angled triangles joined on the diagonal to form a square. These small but mighty blocks can be used to create intricate and complex designs simply by twisting and turning them and mixing up your fabric combinations.

To avoid sewing on bias edges, most quilters make their HSTs two or even eight at a time; you'll learn both methods here. These instructions make slightly oversized blocks to allow for accurate trimming and perfect points – even experienced quilters often prefer to oversize their blocks, as perfectly lining up your squares and diagonal lines every time can be a little tricky.

Two-at-a-time HSTs*

STEP-BY-STEP: HOW TO MAKE TWO-AT-A-TIME HSTS

Step 1: Place your squares right sides together and mark a diagonal line from corner to corner on one side of your paired squares using tailor's chalk or a removable fabric pen as shown.

Step 2: Sew ¼in from each side of the marked line.

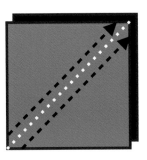

Step 3: Cut along the marked line. Press the seams towards the darker fabric and trim both HSTs to 3½ × 3½in squares.

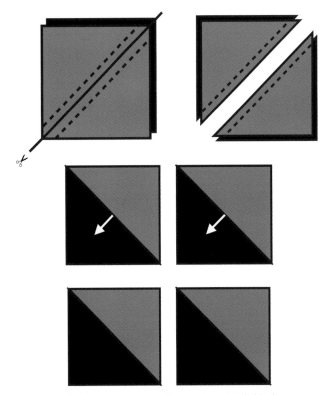

Finished two-at-a-time Half-Square Triangle blocks.

Eight-at-a-time HSTs

TOP TIP

When using large starting squares, use pins to prevent fabric shifting and reduce inaccuracies.

STEP-BY-STEP: HOW TO MAKE EIGHT-AT-A-TIME HSTS

Step 1: Place your squares right sides together and mark diagonal lines from corner to corner on one side of your paired squares using tailor's chalk or a removable fabric pen as shown.

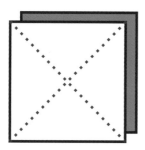

Step 2: Sew ¼in from each side of the marked lines.

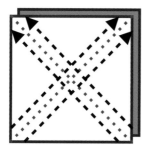

Step 3: Cut the square vertically and horizontally as shown, then along the marked diagonal lines. Press the seams towards the darker fabric (here fabric B) and trim each HST to 3½ × 3½in squares.

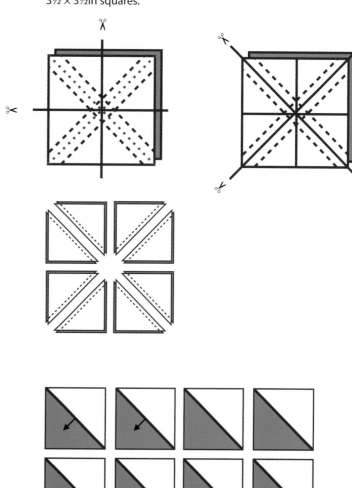

Finished eight-at-a-time Half-Square Triangle blocks.

QUARTER-SQUARE TRIANGLES

Similar in construction to two-at-a-time HSTs, Quarter-Square Triangles (commonly referred to as QSTs) are four right-angle triangles joined along their short edges to form a square. Another extremely versatile block, the QST can be adapted to include four, three or two colours as well as a 'split' version made of three triangles, and you'll be covering each variation here.

To avoid sewing on bias edges, most quilters make their QSTs four at a time by making two sets of HSTs and mixing them together to make the final blocks, and this is the method you're going to learn here. As with HSTs, these instructions make slightly oversized blocks to allow for accurate trimming and perfect points.

YOU WILL NEED

- One 7½ × 7½in square (fabric A)
- One 7½ × 7½in square (fabric B)
- One 7½ × 7½in square (fabric C)
- One 7½ × 7½in square (fabric E)

Finished size: 6 × 6in
Unfinished size: 6½ × 6½in
Makes four blocks

TOP TIP

Make sure to carefully centre your HSTs when nesting in step 4 and draw your guideline at a precise 90-degree angle.

Four-colour QSTs*

STEP-BY-STEP: HOW TO MAKE FOUR-COLOUR QSTS

Step 1: Place one square of fabric A with one square of fabric E, right sides together, and mark a diagonal line from corner to corner on one side of your paired squares using tailor's chalk or a removable fabric pen as shown.

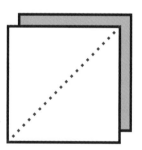

Step 2: Sew ¼in from each side of the marked line. Cut along the marked line and press seams towards fabric E. Do not trim.

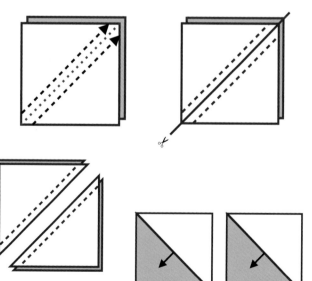

continued on following page...

Step 3: Using fabrics B and C, repeat steps 1 and 2, pressing to fabric B.

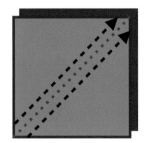

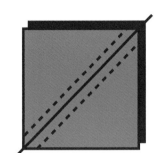

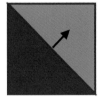

Step 4: Pair one fabric A+E sub-block with one fabric B+C sub-block right sides together as shown and taking care to nest the seams. Mark the opposite diagonal and sew ¼in from either side as shown.

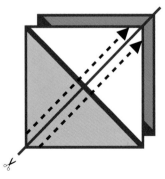

Step 5: Cut along the marked lines. Press seams open and trim to 6½ × 6½in squares, centring the middle of the block at 3¼in.

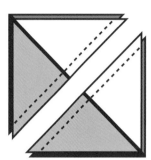

Step 6: Repeat steps 4 and 5 with the second set of sub-blocks.

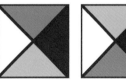

Finished four-colour Quarter-Square Triangle blocks.

Three-colour QSTs*

YOU WILL NEED

- Two 7½ × 7½in squares (fabric A)
- One 7½ × 7½in square (fabric B)
- One 7½ × 7½in square (fabric C)

Finished size: 6 × 6in
Unfinished size: 6½ × 6½in
Makes four blocks

TOP TIP

Pay careful attention to block orientation when aligning your HSTs to stop fabric A triangles ending up next to each other in the final assembly.

STEP-BY-STEP: HOW TO MAKE A THREE-COLOUR QST

Step 1: Place one square of fabric A with one square of fabric B right sides together and mark a diagonal line from corner to corner on one side of your paired squares using tailor's chalk or a removable fabric pen as shown.

Step 2: Sew ¼in from each side of the marked line. Cut along the marked line and press seams towards fabric B. Do not trim.

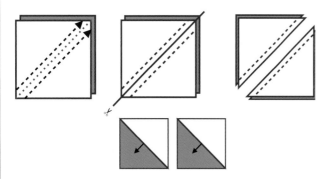

Step 3: Using the second square of fabric A and fabric C, repeat steps 1 and 2, pressing to fabric C.

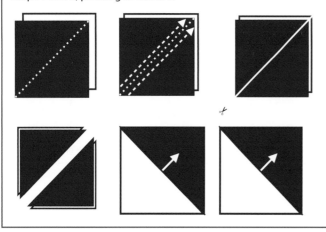

Step 4: Pair one fabric A+B sub-block with one fabric A+C sub-block right sides together as shown and taking care to nest the seams. Mark the opposite diagonal and sew ¼in from each side as shown.

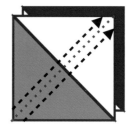

Step 5: Cut along the marked lines. Press seams open and trim each QST to 6½ × 6½in square, centring the middle of the block at 3¼in.

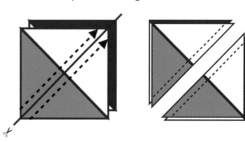

Step 6: Repeat steps 4 and 5 with the second set of sub-blocks.

Finished three-colour Quarter-Square Triangle block.

Two-colour QSTs*

Also known as Hourglass blocks.

- One 7½ × 7½in square (fabric B)
- One 7½ × 7½in square (fabric C)

Finished size: 6 × 6in
Unfinished size: 6½ × 6½in
Makes two blocks

Make sure to press all seams towards fabric C to allow for easy seam nesting.

STEP-BY-STEP: HOW TO MAKE TWO-COLOUR QSTS

Step 1: Place squares of fabric B and fabric C right sides together and mark a diagonal line from corner to corner on one side of your paired squares using tailor's chalk or a removable fabric pen as shown.

Step 2: Sew ¼in from each side of the marked line. Cut along the marked line and press seams towards fabric C. Do not trim.

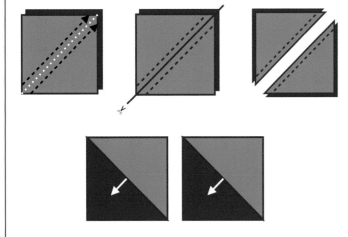

Step 3: Repeat steps 1 and 2 to make a total of four HST sub-blocks.

Step 4: Pair two sub-blocks right sides together as shown and taking care to nest the seams. Mark the opposite diagonal and sew ¼in from each side as shown.

Step 5: Cut along the marked lines. Press seams open and trim each QST to 6½ × 6½in square, centring the middle of the block at 3¼in.

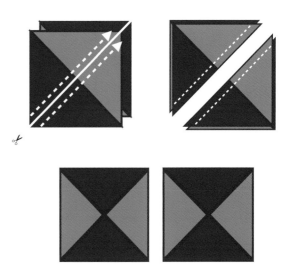

Finished two-colour Quarter-Square Triangle block.

Split QSTs*

Also known as Three-Patch QSTs.

YOU WILL NEED

- Two 7 × 7in squares (fabric B)
- One 7½ × 7½in square (fabric C)
- One 7½ × 7½in square (fabric D)

Finished size: 6 × 6in
Unfinished size: 6½ × 6½in
Makes four blocks

STEP-BY-STEP: HOW TO MAKE SPLIT QSTS

Step 1: Place one square of fabric C with one square of fabric D right sides together and mark a diagonal line from corner to corner on one side of your paired squares using tailor's chalk or a removable fabric pen as shown.

Step 2: Sew ¼in from each side of the marked line. Cut along the marked line and press seam open. Trim to 7 × 7in.

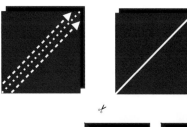

Step 3: Pair fabric C+D sub-block with fabric B square right sides together. Mark the opposite diagonal and sew ¼in from either side as shown.

Step 4: Cut along the marked lines. Press seams open and trim each QST to 6½ × 6½in square, centring the middle of the block at 3¼in.

Step 5: Repeat steps 3 and 4 with the second set of sub-blocks.

Finished Split Quarter-Square Triangle block.

FLYING GEESE

The common name for a 2:1 (twice as wide as it is high) rectangle block containing a triangle reminiscent of the V shape made by a flock of geese in flight. This block is a little controversial in the quilt world, as there is division over whether one of these blocks is called Flying Geese or Flying Goose, but as most people agree that it is a great block, you can pick the name you prefer!

While Flying Geese can be made one at a time, to speed up the process of making them, many quilters make their Flying Geese blocks four at a time; you'll learn both methods here. As these blocks can be a little tricky to sew accurately, these instructions will produce slightly oversized blocks to allow for easier trimming and sharper points.

One-at-a-time Flying Geese*

Sometimes called the 'stitch and flip' method (you first encountered this technique in the Snowball Corners block).

YOU WILL NEED

- Two 3½ × 3½in squares (fabric C)
- One 3½ × 6½in rectangle (fabric E)

Finished size: 3 × 6in
Unfinished size: 3½ × 6½in
Makes one block

TOP TIP

Make sure you leave a ¼in seam allowance from the top point when trimming to prevent blunt-nosed geese when your blocks are assembled.

STEP-BY-STEP: HOW TO MAKE ONE-AT-A-TIME FLYING GEESE

Step 1: Place one square of fabric A right sides together with the left-hand side of fabric B rectangle and mark a diagonal line from corner to corner on one side of your paired squares using tailor's chalk or a removable fabric pen as shown.

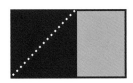

Step 2: Sew along the marked line and trim excess to ¼in seam allowance. Press to fabric A.

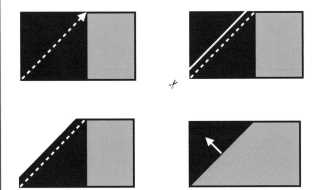

Step 3: Repeat on the other side of fabric B rectangle as shown. Press seam to fabric A and trim to 3½ × 6½in.

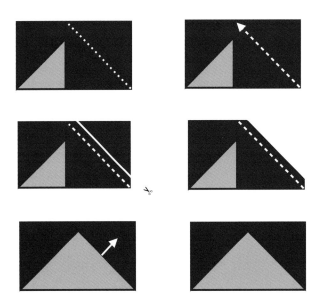

Finished one-at-a-time Flying Geese block.

Four-at-a-time Flying Geese

Sometimes called the 'no waste' method.

- Four 4 × 4in squares (fabric A)
- One 7½ × 7½in square (fabric B)

Finished size: 3 × 6in
Unfinished size: 3½ × 6½in
Makes four blocks

Make sure you leave a ¼in seam allowance from the top point when trimming to prevent blunt-nosed geese when your blocks are assembled.

STEP-BY-STEP: HOW TO MAKE FOUR-AT-A-TIME FLYING GEESE

Step 1: Place two squares of fabric A right sides together in opposite corners of the fabric B square and mark a diagonal line from corner to corner on one side of your paired squares using tailor's chalk or a removable fabric pen as shown.

Note: the smaller squares will overlap slightly when correctly positioned.

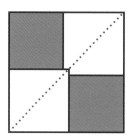

Step 2: Sew ¼in from each side of the marked line. Cut along the marked line and press seams towards fabric A.

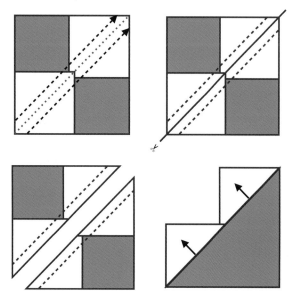

Step 3: Place one square of fabric A right sides together with the corner of each sub-block as shown and mark a diagonal line.

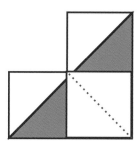

Step 4: Sew ¼in from each side of the marked line. Cut along the marked line and press seams towards fabric A.

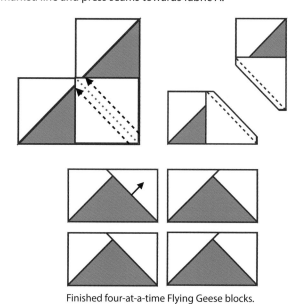

Finished four-at-a-time Flying Geese blocks.

Step 5: Repeat steps 3–4 with the other sub-block.

Step 6: Trim to 3½ × 6½in.

HALF-RECTANGLE TRIANGLES*

Half-Rectangle Triangles (or HRTS as they are often known) are like Half-Square Triangles, just with a twist. Formed of two right-angled triangles joined on the diagonal to form a 2:1 (twice as high as it is wide) rectangle, these blocks are often sewn two at a time to avoid sewing bias edges. These instructions make slightly oversized blocks to allow for accurate trimming and perfect points – even experienced quilters often prefer to oversize these blocks, as perfectly lining up your rectangles and diagonal lines can be tricky.

STEP-BY-STEP: HOW TO MAKE HALF-RECTANGLE TRIANGLES (HRTS)

Step 1: Place your rectangles right sides together and twist so that the top left corner of fabric E matches the top right corner of fabric B, and the bottom right corner of fabric E matches the bottom left corner of fabric B.

Step 2: Mark a diagonal line from corner to corner on one side of the fabric E rectangle using tailor's chalk or a removable fabric pen as shown.

Step 3: Sew ¼in from either side of the marked line.

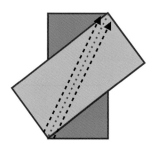

Step 4: Cut along the marked lines. Press the seams towards fabric E and trim each HRT to 3½ × 6½in rectangles.

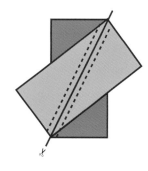
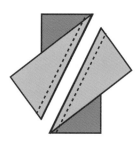
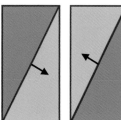
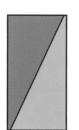

Finished Half-Rectangle Triangle blocks.

SQUARE-IN-A-SQUARE

The Square-in-a-Square (SIAS) block is also known as the Diamond-in-a-Square block or an Economy block (a name thought to date back to the Great Depression of the 1930s when smaller cuts of fabric were used economically to create quilts and bedding). While it can be expanded indefinitely with extra rounds to make square-in-a-square-in-a-square and so on, typically it is used in the single and double forms. This block can be made in a variety of ways, including the stitch and flip and triangles methods you'll cover here.

Single Square-in-a-Square: Stitch and flip method

TOP TIP

If your corner squares are big enough, sew another line ½in away from the main stitching line so that when you trim the corner off, you have ready-made Half-Square Triangles to use in another project.

STEP-BY-STEP: HOW TO USE THE STITCH AND FLIP METHOD TO MAKE A SINGLE SIAS

Step 1: Place two squares of fabric A right sides together in opposite corners of the fabric B square and mark a diagonal line from corner to corner on one side of your paired squares using tailor's chalk or a removable fabric pen as shown.

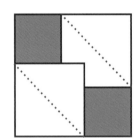

Note: The smaller squares will overlap slightly when correctly positioned.

Step 2: Sew along the marked lines and trim excess to ¼in seam allowance. Press to fabric A.

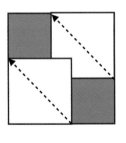
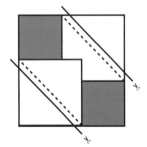
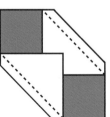
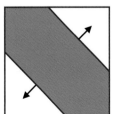

Step 3: Sew remaining fabric A squares to opposite sides of the sub-block, trimming excess to ¼in seam allowance and pressing seams towards fabric A.

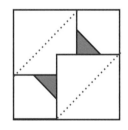
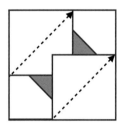
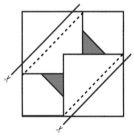
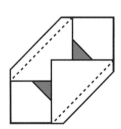
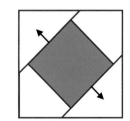
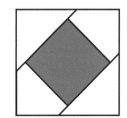

Finished Single Square-in-a-Square (stitch and flip method) block.

Single Square-in-a-Square: Triangles Method*

- One 4¾ × 4¾in square (fabric B)
- One 3⅞ × 3⅞in square cut in half diagonally (fabric A)
- One 3⅞ × 3⅞in square cut in half diagonally (fabric E)

Finished size: 6 × 6in
Unfinished size: 6½ × 6½in
Makes one block

- Make sure you have ¼in seam allowance from each point when trimming to prevent blunt corners when your blocks are assembled.
- Fold triangles and square in half and finger press a small crease at the mid-point to help when aligning.

STEP-BY-STEP: HOW TO USE THE TRIANGLES METHOD TO MAKE A SINGLE SIAS

Step 1: Sew two fabric E triangles to opposite sides of the fabric B square as shown. Press seams open and do *not* trim.

Step 2: Sew fabric A triangles to opposite sides of the sub-block, pressing seams open. Trim to 6½ × 6½in.

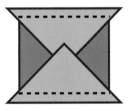 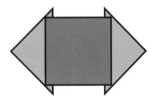 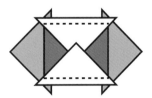 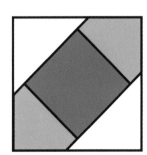

Finished Single Square-in-a-Square (triangles method) block.

Double Square-in-a-Square*

- One 3½ × 3½in square (fabric C)
- Two 3 × 3in squares cut in half diagonally (fabric B)
- One 3⅞ × 3⅞in square cut in half diagonally (fabric A)

- One 3⅞ × 3⅞in square cut in half diagonally (fabric D)

Finished size: 6 × 6in
Unfinished size: 6½ × 6½in
Makes one block

- Make sure you have ¼in seam allowance from each point when trimming in steps 2 and 4 to prevent blunt corners.
- Fold triangles and square in half and finger press a small crease at the mid-point to help when aligning.

STEP-BY-STEP: HOW TO MAKE A DOUBLE SIAS

Step 1: Sew two fabric B triangles to opposite sides of fabric C square as shown. Press seams open and do *not* trim.

 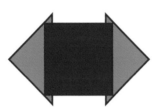

Step 2: Sew remaining fabric B triangles to opposite sides of the sub-block, pressing seams open. Trim to 4¾ × 4¾in.

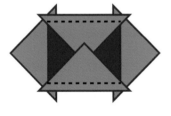 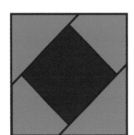

Step 3: Sew two fabric A triangles to opposite sides of assembled sub-block as shown. Press seams open and do not trim.

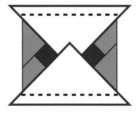 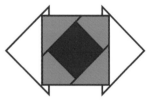

Step 4: Sew fabric D triangles to opposite sides of the sub-block, pressing seams open. Trim to 6½ × 6½in.

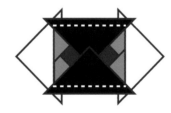 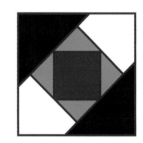

Finished Double Square-in-a-Square block.

LOG CABIN*

A classic quilt block made by adding strips in a clockwise direction around a central square, this block can be added to indefinitely to make large blocks and even whole quilt tops. These blocks are excellent for using up long strips of fabric and look wonderful when made from a mix of patterns and colours.

TOP TIP

Press carefully with an iron after adding each rectangle, taking care not to warp the fabric out of shape as this will make accurate sewing more difficult.

YOU WILL NEED

- One 2½ × 2½in square of fabric B
- One 1½ × 2½in rectangle of fabric D
- Two 1½ × 3½in rectangles of fabric A
- One 1½ × 4½in rectangle of fabric D
- One 1½ × 4½in rectangle of fabric C
- Two 1½ × 5½in rectangles of fabric E
- One 1½ × 6½in rectangle of fabric C

Finished size: 6 × 6in
Unfinished size: 6½ × 6½in
Makes one block

STEP-BY-STEP: HOW TO MAKE A LOG CABIN

Step 1: With right sides together, sew 1½ × 2½in rectangle of fabric D to the top of the fabric B square. Press seam open.

Step 2: Join 1½ × 3½in rectangle of fabric A to the right of the assembled sub-block, pressing seam open.

Step 3: Join 1½ × 3½in rectangle of fabric A to the bottom of the assembled sub-block, pressing seams open.

Step 4: Continuing to work in a clockwise direction, pressing seam open, and join the remainder of fabric C, D and E rectangles in the order shown.

Finished Log Cabin block.

QUARTER LOG CABIN*

A variation on the Log Cabin block, a Quarter Log Cabin block works only on one corner of the square by adding strips to the top and right in turn and expanding as far as required. This block offers some exciting visual possibilities when spun in different directions and it is worth taking time to play with your design.

TOP TIP

Press carefully with an iron after adding each rectangle, taking care not to warp the fabric out of shape as this will make accurate sewing more difficult.

YOU WILL NEED

- One 2½ × 2½in square of fabric A
- One 1½ × 2½in rectangle of fabric B
- One 1½ × 3½in rectangle of fabric B
- One 1½ × 3½in rectangle of fabric C
- One 1½ × 4½in rectangle of fabric C
- One 1½ × 4½in rectangle of fabric D
- One 1½ × 5½in rectangle of fabric D
- One 1½ × 5½in rectangle of fabric E
- One 1½ × 6½in rectangle of fabric E

Finished size: 6 × 6in
Unfinished size: 6½ × 6½in
Makes one block

STEP-BY-STEP: HOW TO MAKE A QUARTER LOG CABIN

Step 1: With right sides together, sew 1½ × 2½in rectangle of fabric B to the top of your fabric A square. Press the seam open.

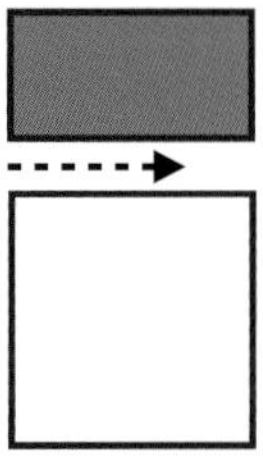

Step 2: Join 1½ × 3½in rectangle of fabric B to the right of the assembled sub-block, pressing the seam open.

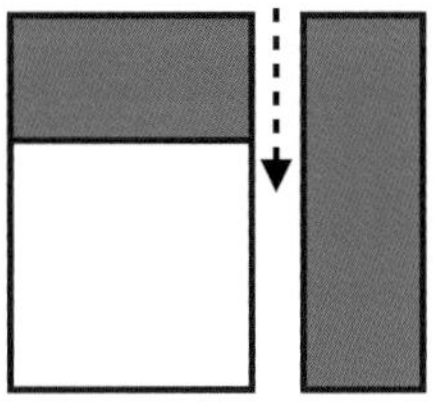

Step 3: Following the same sequence of joining to the top and then the right of the growing sub-block, join the remainder of fabric C, D and E rectangles in the order shown. Press seams open.

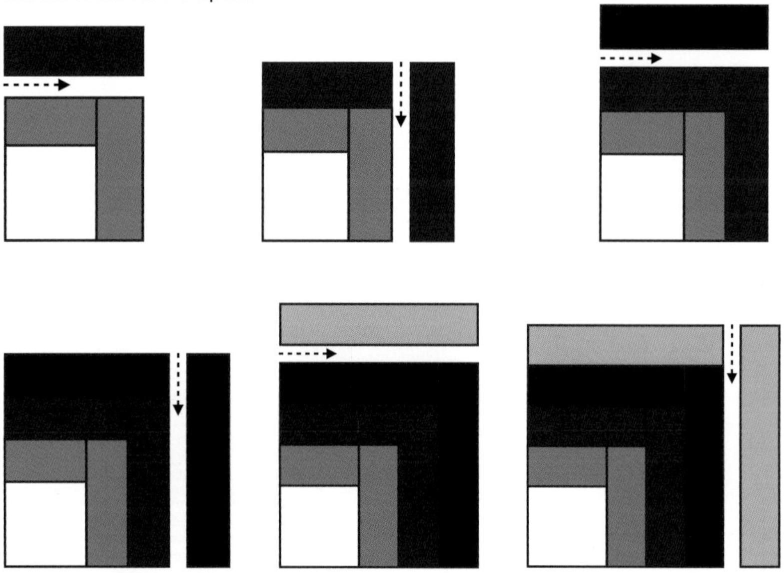

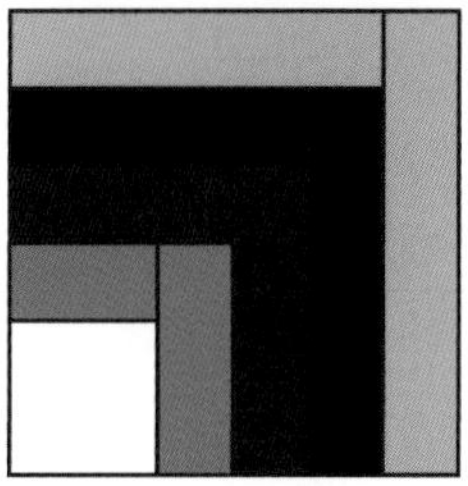

Finished Quarter Log Cabin block.

COURTHOUSE STEPS*

Another variation of the Log Cabin block, the Courthouse Steps block is built by adding strips to opposite sides of a central square, working outwards to the top and bottom, then left and right. Using a mix of light and dark fabrics can create a wide variety of striking visual effects, especially when joining blocks together.

YOU WILL NEED

- One 2½ × 2½in square of fabric B
- Two 1½ × 2½in rectangles of fabric E
- Two 1½ × 4½in rectangles of fabric C
- Two 1½ × 4½in rectangles of fabric A
- Two 1½ × 6½in rectangles of fabric B

Finished size: 6 × 6in
Unfinished size: 6½ × 6½in
Makes one block

STEP-BY-STEP: HOW TO MAKE COURTHOUSE STEPS

Step 1: With right sides together, sew 1½ × 2½in rectangles of fabric E to the left and right of your fabric B square. Press the seams open.

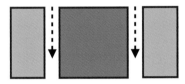

Step 2: Join 1½ × 4½in rectangles of fabric C to the top and bottom of the assembled sub-block, pressing the seams open.

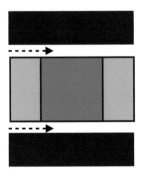

Step 3: Following the same sequence of joining to the top and bottom and then the left and right of the growing sub-block, join the remainder of fabric A and B rectangles in the order shown. Press seams open.

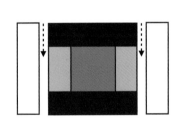
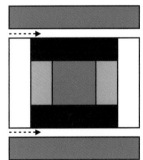

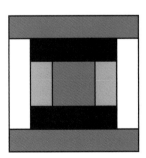

Finished Courthouse Steps block.

TRIANGLES*

While triangles of any shape and size can be pieced together with enough patience and practice, the most common non-right-angled triangles found in quilting are isosceles triangles. These have the benefit of tessellating nicely into neat and even rows, and by varying colour and pattern placement you can create some truly stunning and intricate-looking quilts with quite simple piecing.

YOU WILL NEED

- One 3½ × 12in rectangle (fabric B)
- One 3½ × 12in rectangle (fabric E)
- One sampler Triangle block template

Finished size: 6 × 6in
Unfinished size: 6½ × 6½in
Makes one block

TOP TIPS

- Pay careful attention to the rotation and order of the triangles when piecing and make sure to line up the angled points from the template to help achieve precise points when joining rows together.
- When working with bias edges, minimise how much you handle the cut pieces to avoid stretching them out of shape.
- Sew slowly and pin the points to help keep things neat and accurate.

STEP-BY-STEP: HOW TO SEW TRIANGLES

Step 1: Using the Triangle block template, cut five each of fabric B and fabric E from the 3½ × 12in rectangles. When cutting triangles, rotate the template as shown, aligning sides to reduce waste and maximise triangles cut per strip.

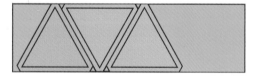

Step 2: With right sides together, form rows in the order shown. Press seams as shown before attaching the next triangle.

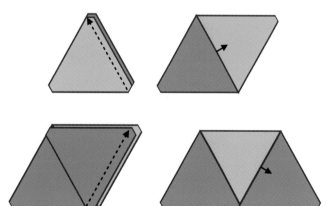

Step 3: With right sides together, join your rows along the long edge, taking care to nest seams. Press the final seam open.

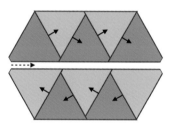

Step 4: Trim the assembled block to 6½ × 6½in as shown, discarding the trimmed edges.

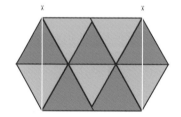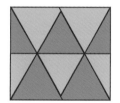

Finished Triangles block.

CURVES

Curves come in many shapes and sizes, and while they may look intimidating at first glance, they aren't as scary as they seem. Whether you're making Quarter Circles, Orange Peels or Inset Circles, the key with curves is to take your time, go slowly and give everything a good press when you're done – you'll be amazed at how much better your block looks when it's been pressed.

You're going to cover the pinning technique here as this is the easiest starting point for dipping your toes into the world of curves, but you could easily swap pins for temporary fabric glue if you'd prefer to avoid pins or find them tricky to use.

Note: The curves templates in this book have two seam allowance options – cut along the dotted line for an exact ¼in seam allowance or around the solid grey shape for a more generous ½in seam allowance that gives room for error and accurate trimming.

Quarter Circles*

Also known as Drunkard's Path blocks after the meandering path of someone intoxicated, Quarter Circles are the easiest curves to sew.

TOP TIP

Sew slowly and check your seams as you sew to make sure there are no gathers or tucks in your fabric.

STEP-BY-STEP: HOW TO MAKE QUARTER CIRCLES

Step 1: Cut one template A from fabric C and one template B from fabric B. Fold each in half and finger press a small crease at the midpoint of the curved edge.

Step 2: With right sides together and matching creases, pin pieces together at the crease as shown.

Step 3: Working from the outside edges in, pin together roughly every 1in, ensuring the straight edges of template B align with the short edges of template A.

Step 4: Using a ¼in seam, slowly sew along the curved edge, removing pins as you go.

Step 5: Press the seam open and trim the block to 6½ × 6½in.

Finished Quarter Circle block.

Orange Peel*

The next step in your curves journey, the Orange Peel block, is formed by sewing two curved seams from corner to corner of a square to create a leaf or petal shape in the centre of the block.

YOU WILL NEED

- One 7 × 7in square (fabric B)
- One 8 × 8in square (fabric E)
- One each of Orange Peel templates A & B

Finished size: 6 × 6in
Unfinished size: 6½ × 6½in
Makes one block

TOP TIP

Sew slowly and check your seams as you sew to make sure there are no gathers or tucks in your fabric.

STEP-BY-STEP: HOW TO MAKE ORANGE PEEL

Step 1: Cut one Orange Peel template A from fabric B and two of Orange Peel template B from fabric E. Fold each in half and finger press a small crease at the mid-point of the curved edge.

Step 2: With right sides together and matching creases, pin fabric B and one fabric E piece together at the crease as shown.

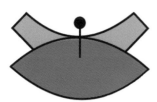

Step 3: Working from the outside edges in, pin together roughly every 1in, ensuring the straight edges of fabric E align with the short ends of template A.

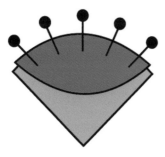

Step 4: Using a ¼in seam, slowly sew along the curved edge, removing pins as you go.

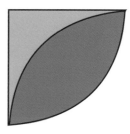

Step 5: Press the seam open. Repeat with the second fabric E piece on the opposite side of the sub-block, and trim block to 6½× 6½in.

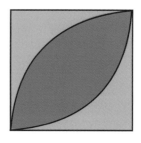

Finished Orange Peel block.

Inset Circles

Instead of cutting a circle into quarters and joining four sub-blocks to create a full circle, by sewing inset circles you can add a full circle into the centre of your quilt block.

YOU WILL NEED

- One 13½ × 13½in square (fabric A)
- One 8 × 8in square (fabric B)
- One each of Inset Circle templates A & B

Finished size: 12 × 12in
Unfinished size: 12½ × 12½in
Makes one block

TOP TIP

Sew slowly (turning down your machine speed if needed) and handle the cut fabric very gently to prevent warping and a block that will not lie flat when pressed.

STEP-BY-STEP: HOW TO MAKE INSET CIRCLES

Step 1: Fold your squares into quarters and cut one Inset Circle template A from fabric A and one Inset Circle template B from fabric B, taking care to align the corner of the template with the folded corner of your fabric as shown.

Step 2: Finger press a small crease at the quarter points of the curved edges.

Step 3: With right sides together and matching creases, pin fabric A and fabric B together at the creases as shown.

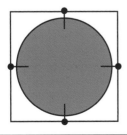

Step 4: Working from the outside edges in, pin together roughly every 1in ensuring that there are no gathers or tucks.

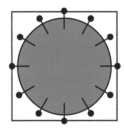

Step 5: Using a ¼in seam, slowly sew around the circle removing pins as you go and taking care not to pull your fabric out of shape. Sew over your original starting point by approximately ¼in to secure your threads and backstitch two to four stitches.

Step 6: Carefully press the seam towards fabric A and trim to 12½ × 12½in.

Finished Inset Circle block.

ENGLISH PAPER PIECING

English Paper Piecing (commonly called EPP) is an incredibly versatile hand-sewing technique that is very portable, great for creating precise shapes and using up scraps. Despite dating back to the 1700s, the final look of an English Paper Pieced quilt can be as modern or traditional as you want, depending on your fabric and pattern choices.

In EPP, fabric is folded around paper templates to create crisp and precise shapes which are then hand stitched together before later removing the papers. While slower than machine piecing, with EPP you can get perfectly precise corners and matching points very simply and it can easily be done on the sofa while watching TV and snuggling under the quilt top before it's even finished. EPP is also great for fussy cutting (also known as meticulous cutting and precision cutting), which is the careful cutting of fabric to include a specific section or motif of your fabric's pattern. This technique can be used to great effect in creating kaleidoscopes and making a feature of specific parts of a fabric's print.

This block uses hexagons (or hexies as they're commonly called) as they're the easiest beginner shape with no tricky acute angles or curved edges to contend with while you get to grips with the technique, but you can sew any shapes you want using this technique, even curves.

YOU WILL NEED

- One fat eighth (F8) of fabric A
- One fat eighth (F8) of fabric B
- One fat eighth (F8) of fabric C
- One hexie fabric cutting template
- Forty-six copies of hexie papers template (make five copies of full-page hexie paper templates)

Finished size: 9½ × 9½in
Unfinished size: 10 × 10in
Makes one block

TOP TIPS

- If you trace or cut the piecing templates inaccurately your pieces will not fit together, so take your time on this step.
- Copy the templates onto thin printer paper or card, but do not use thick card stock. You can reuse your EPP papers multiple times once they have been removed from the fabric.

STEP-BY-STEP: HOW TO CUT HEXIES

Step 1: Using the hexie fabric cutting template, cut out a fabric hexie using your preferred method:

Method 1: Laying the fabric cutting template over your fabric, mark the outline of the template, remove the template and cut around the outline using scissors or rotary cutter.

 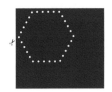

Method 2: Holding the template in place, use a rotary cutter or scissors to cut out without marking.

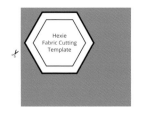

Step 2: Repeat so you have 46 fabric hexies cut out in the following distribution:

- Fabric A × 18
- Fabric B × 14
- Fabric C × 14

Step 3: Taking care to be very accurate, cut out 46 copies of the hexie paper template.

STEP-BY-STEP: HOW TO BASTE HEXIES

Step 1: Tack your cut hexies wrong sides together with the paper pattern pieces using your preferred method:

Method 1 (glue basting): Draw a small line of temporary sewing glue on the wrong side of your fabric along each side of the hexie. Fold over the seam allowance of each side in turn (1–6) making sure that the fabric folds exactly along the edge of the paper template.

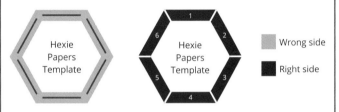

Method 2 (thread basting): Folding each side carefully over in turn (1–6), use long tacking stitches running from corner to corner to secure the fabric to the template.

Note: When basted, your fabric should be right side out on one side of the paper template – this is the fabric that will show in your assembled quilt top.

TOP TIP

If you find you have some skinny seams, readjust your paper template to make sure that you have ¼in seam allowance for each edge.

STEP-BY-STEP: HOW TO JOIN HEXIES

Step 1: Placing two basted hexies RST, insert your needle between the paper and seam allowance of the top hexie approximately 2mm from your starting corner (hiding your thread knot between the layers). Whip stitch to the corner, taking care to only catch the top one to three threads of each hexie fabric then work back across to the opposite corner.

Step 2: Sew hexies together in the order and along the stitching lines shown, folding the hexies as needed to ensure you are always sewing along a flat edge.

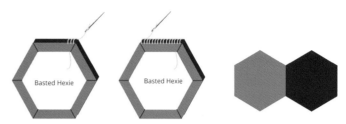

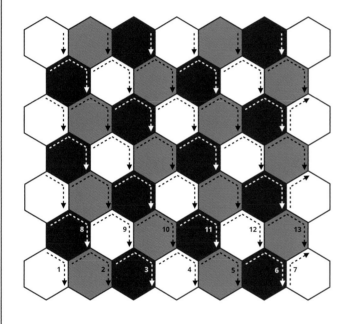

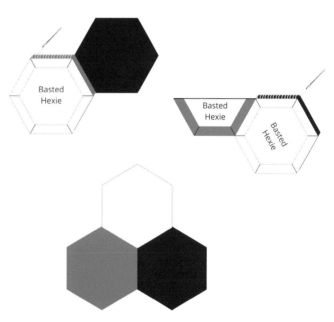

TOP TIPS

- To secure your thread at the end of a section or when changing thread, bring your needle up in the seam allowance (away from the edges) and either make a small knot or do three to four small stitches in place to secure and trim thread tail.
- When cutting your thread, as a rule of thumb you should never cut a length longer than that of your thumb to the centre of your chest. This will help keep the thread at a manageable length and reduce the likelihood of it knotting or snagging.
- Take care to ensure your hexies are correctly placed and orientated before starting to sew.

Step 1: Remove the papers once every adjoining piece is securely sewn together. This can be done as you go or all together once the whole block is assembled.

Step 2: Trim the assembled block as shown to measure 10 × 10in, discarding the trimmed sides.

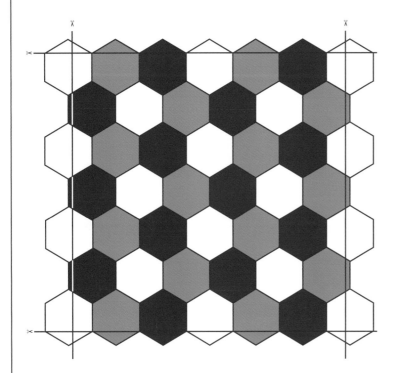

Finished English Paper Piecing block.

FOUNDATION PAPER PIECING

Foundation Paper Piecing (commonly called FPP) is perfect for creating super precise and detailed designs. FPP uses machine stitching to sew fabric to paper templates (which are later removed), building up intricate shapes with ease and avoiding potentially tricky-to-sew partial and Y-seams.

TOP TIP

To make piecing easier, pre-fold the template along the solid stitch lines using a postcard or thin ruler before you begin to sew.

STEP-BY-STEP: HOW TO CUT FPP BLOCKS

Step 1: Cut out the templates including the ¼in seam allowances (shown as a dotted line).

Step 2: Lay template A on the wrong side of the fabric to be used in section A1. Folding back template sections A2 and A3 as needed, cut around the outline of section A1 plus an additional ½in seam allowance. Repeat for remaining template A, B and C sections.

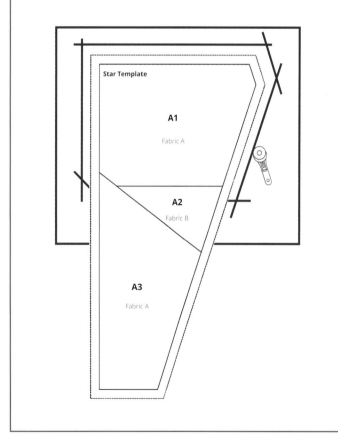

Star Template

A1
Fabric A

A2
Fabric B

A3
Fabric A

Step 1: With fabric right side facing away from the template, place cut A1 piece on the reverse of template A and pin in place. Place A2 right sides together with piece A1 and align along the seam line, pinning in place.

Step 2: Using a short stitch (1.2–1.5mm), sew along the length of the A1–A2 seam line being careful not to stitch into joining section. Backstitch two stitches at the beginning and end of each line to secure.

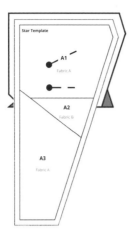

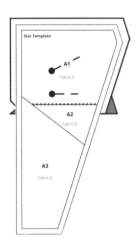

Front view.

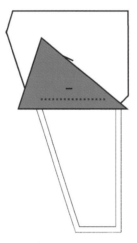

Back view.

Step 3: Fold the paper template back along the sewn line, trim the seam to ¼in and press fabric pieces open.

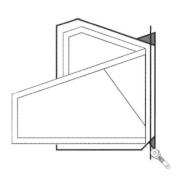

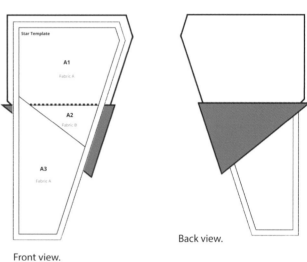

Front view.

Back view.

Step 4: Fold the paper back along the A2–A3 seam line and trim fabric to ¼in seam allowance.

Step 5: Continue piecing following the suggested order (A1, A2, A3). Press the whole block and trim to the edge of the template (keeping the seam allowance).

Step 6: Repeat with templates B and C.

- Use a light box or hold the piece up to a light to ensure you have a minimum of ¼in seam allowance around the section you are piecing.
- Remove the paper covering the seam allowance before joining the template for easier paper removal.

STEP-BY-STEP: ASSEMBLING THE PPP STAR

Step 1: When you have pieced each of the templates, assemble the block by lining up the pattern templates right sides together and matching the points in the following order:
A + B + C

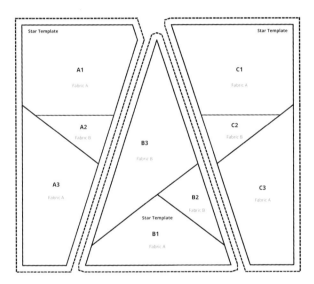

Step 2: Gently remove the papers and press the block.

Finished Foundation Paper Piecing block.

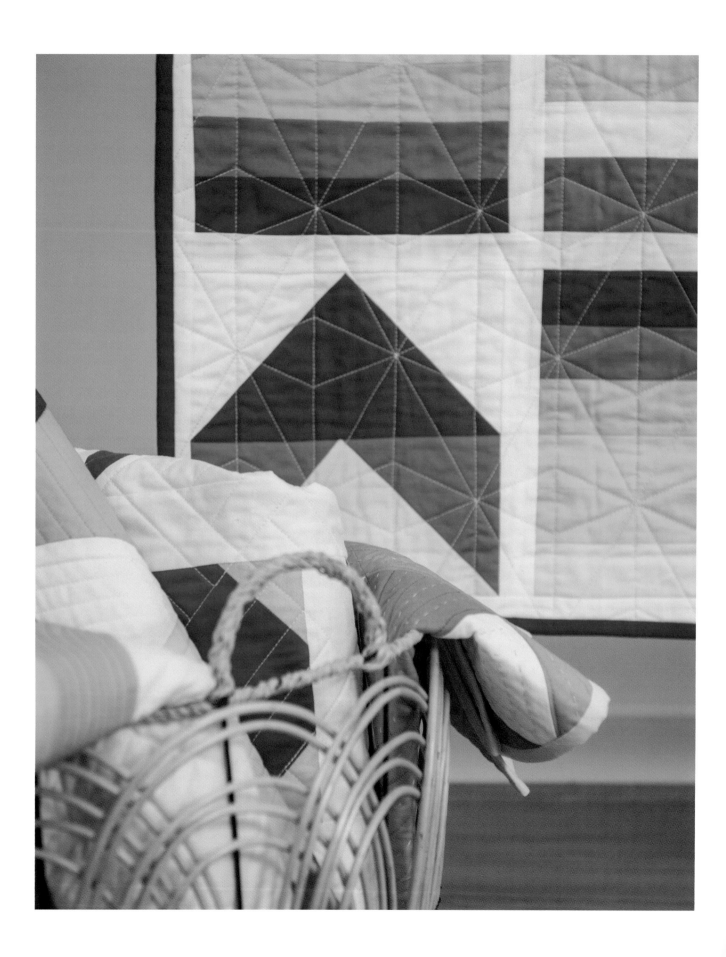

CHAPTER 6

FINISHING YOUR QUILT

You've made a quilt top – what next? It's all too easy to fall into the trap of making endless quilt tops and never finishing them for fear of 'messing them up', 'ruining them' or just not finishing them quite 'perfectly' enough. If you find yourself falling into that trap, remember that *all* quilts are perfectly imperfect (yes, really, even award-winning quilts have some tiny flaws only the maker notices) and that finished is better than perfect, especially when you're hoping to snuggle under it for warmth in winter or gift it to a loved one.

Now you've decided to finish your quilt top, you might be wondering what that involves. This chapter will walk you through the key stages of finishing a quilt from basting to quilting and binding, as well as offering you a few different options for each to help you find what works best for you.

BACKING

The first step towards finishing your quilt is to decide on your backing. This is the fabric layer on the reverse of the quilt, and you have two options for backing: wholecloth or pieced. The backing of a quilt is often overlooked when it comes to fabric choices, but as a two-sided creation it is worth putting thought into the back as well as the front. Consider which fabrics and colours will complement the front the most. A bold modern print? A solid colour matching the quilt top? A soft flannel checked print? The possibilities are endless and there is no right answer – if you love it, it's perfect.

A pieced backing from scraps adds a fun visual design element to the reverse of this quilt, especially with the quilting design showing so clearly.

The backing fabric for Constellation was chosen both as a complementary colour and as a way of adding some whimsy to the quilt.

It's important to bear in mind when choosing which option to go for that your backing will need to be around 6in wider and longer than your quilt top to allow for spreading and movement during the quilting stage. If you're long arm quilting your quilt, the backing might need to be even larger.

Depending on the size of your quilt, standard yardage might be wide enough to cut the required length without any piecing required and this is the simplest option available to you. Typically quilts that finish up to around 36–38in on one side (generally baby-size quilts and smaller) can be backed using standard 42in wide yardage. For example, if your quilt finishes at 36 × 42in you could cut a length the width of fabric (WOF) × 48in long and that would fit perfectly.

If your quilt is wider than WOF or you want to use smaller cuts of fabric that you already have (perhaps a fat quarter bundle you've been holding on to), a pieced backing is the next option. This can be as simple as cutting the largest sections possible from your fabric and joining them together to form the required size, or you could get more creative and add a design element to your backing. 'Improv' backing is growing in popularity and is a great way to use fabric from your stash, scraps and spare quilt blocks to make what is essentially a double-sided quilt. When joining large sections of fabric together, ½in seams pressed open are typically used to improve durability and reduce bulk across the quilt back.

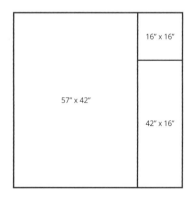

An example of piecing a backing for a 51 × 51in quilt.

If your quilt is too wide for WOF yardage but you also don't want to piece a back, or if you simply want to cut costs (buying yardage to back a queen-size quilt can be rather pricy), a great alternative is to use new or used cotton bed sheets. If you want to use brushed cotton or flannel to add an extra cosiness to a winter quilt, bed sheets are often a more cost-effective way to go about it as flannel can be pricier than standard quilting cotton.

BASTING

Once you have your backing sorted, it's time to baste your quilt. So, what is basting and why does it matter? During the quilting process the layers of the quilt inevitably shift while you move the quilt through your machine. Basting temporarily secures all the layers in place as steadily as possible to prevent slippage and folds or creases being accidentally sewn into your quilt (this is most common on the reverse where you can't see it easily). Bear in mind that your batting will need to be around 6in wider and longer than your quilt top to allow for spreading and movement during the quilting stage.

When the layers of a quilt are layered ready for basting and quilting, they are called a quilt sandwich: the quilt top and backing on the outside and the batting as the filling. There are three main methods for securing the layers together for quilting: thread basting, pin basting and spray basting. It is very common for quilters to switch back and forth between different methods according to their needs as each method has positives and negatives, so it is recommended to try each method at least once to find which works best for you in different circumstances.

TOP TIPS

- If your batting has scrim, a light layer of woven fibres added to some battings to act as a stabiliser and hold the fibres together while quilting (*see* Chapter 3 for a full discussion of batting types), the scrim should be facing the quilt backing rather than the quilt top to reduce bearding during quilting (bearding is the effect of batting fibres passing through to the top of a quilt, leaving a pale fuzz).
- Press your quilt top before basting, especially if you have pieced using the English Paper Piecing method.
- Use masking tape/painter's tape to hold your quilt backing in place as it holds well and can be easily removed without leaving a sticky residue.

Spray basting

Spray basting is arguably the quickest and easiest method and is rapidly becoming the most popular among quilters. A temporary fabric glue is sprayed between the layers of a quilt sandwich to hold them in place during quilting. The most used brand is Odif 505 spray, but others are available – just check that they are a temporary adhesive and suitable for use on fabric before using.

POSITIVES:

- Quick to use.
- Easy to adjust the layers of your quilt sandwich.
- Nothing to remove after quilting.

NEGATIVES:

- You need good ventilation when using the spray to protect your airways.
- Less environmentally friendly than other methods due to the solvents used.
- Expensive – one large can is typically sufficient for three to four medium-sized quilts at most.

STEP-BY-STEP: HOW TO SPRAY BASTE YOUR QUILT

Step 1: Smooth out your quilt backing to remove creases and tape in position to prevent movement.

Step 2: Smooth your batting over the backing, removing any creases and ensuring that it lines up neatly with your backing.

Step 3: Carefully fold back half of the batting and spray temporary adhesive in a section across the width of the quilt. Gently smooth the batting back into place over the sprayed section, ensuring there are no creases in either the backing or batting.

Step 4: Repeat with the rest of the batting, working in sections until all the batting has been sprayed and glued to the backing and there are no creases or folds.

Step 5: Smooth the quilt top over the batting, squaring it up and removing creases. As with the batting, fold the quilt top back and spray adhesive in sections until the whole quilt top is glued and neatly smoothed out.

Step 6: Quilt your quilt!

Pin basting

Pin basting is another quick and easy way of basting, although not quite as speedy as using spray adhesive. The layers of the quilt sandwich are held together by inserting curved safety pins and clipping them closed to hold the layers in place until quilted. Curved pins are used as the bend allows the pin to pass through the width of the quilt layers without puckering or shifting the fabric and batting too much in a way that would add creases to your finished quilt.

POSITIVES:

- The layers are all attached together in a single pass.
- Pins are generally quick and easy to insert.
- Environmentally friendly – the pins are almost infinitely reusable.

NEGATIVES:

- Opening and closing the pins can be tricky, especially if you have reduced strength or mobility in your hands.
- They need to be removed as you sew – you can't sew over them.
- You need a lot of pins for large quilts.

TOP TIP

If you know there are certain places or lines you'll be quilting, try to place your pins to either side to prevent having to stop and start often as you quilt.

STEP-BY-STEP: HOW TO PIN BASTE YOUR QUILT

Step 1: Smooth out your quilt backing to remove creases and tape in position to prevent movement.

Step 2: Smooth your batting over the backing, removing any creases and ensuring that it lines up neatly with your backing.

Step 3: Smooth the quilt top over the batting, squaring it up and removing creases.

Step 4: Starting in the middle and smoothing outwards as you go, insert pins every 4–6in to secure the quilt sandwich.

Step 5: Quilt your quilt, removing any pins in the path of your quilting lines as you go.

Thread basting

Thread basting is the slowest method of basting, but that doesn't mean it should be discounted. The layers of the quilt sandwich are held together with temporary stitches called tailor's tacks which are removed after quilting.

POSITIVES:

- You can easily sew over the tailor's tacks.
- Quick to remove – just snip and pull out the threads.
- No chemicals or sharp points to contend with while quilting.

NEGATIVES:

- Slow to insert compared to other basting methods.
- Not the most environmentally friendly option due to thread wastage.
- Can be tricky to insert if you have reduced strength or mobility in your hands.

STEP-BY-STEP: HOW TO THREAD BASTE YOUR QUILT

Step 1: Smooth out your quilt backing to remove creases and tape in position to prevent movement.

Step 2: Smooth your batting over the backing, removing any creases and ensuring that it lines up neatly with your backing.

Step 3: Smooth the quilt top over the batting, squaring it up and removing creases.

Step 4: Starting in the middle and smoothing outwards as you go, insert a tacking stitch as shown every 4–6in to secure the quilt sandwich.

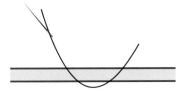

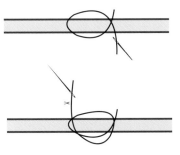

Step 5: Quilt your quilt! Remove the tacking stitches once you've finished.

TOP TIPS

- Using a curved upholstery needle can make step 4 easier as you can loop through the layers of the quilt sandwich more easily.
- Don't use your good thread for this type of basting as it'll just be thrown away after quilting – use the cheapest you have to hand.

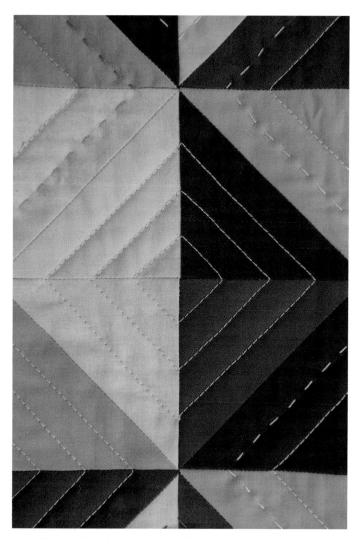

A combination of hand quilting and machine quilting can be very effective and add depth to your quilting design.

The hand-quilting threads here were chosen to complement the rainbow gradation in the design and add an extra visual element.

QUILTING

After basting comes quilting, which is where the magic really happens. While lots of quilters use the term 'quilting' interchangeably to mean both the piecing stage as well as the stage where you join the quilt sandwich together, this section focusses on the latter.

Quilting can be done either by machine or by hand and, depending on your design and thread choices, the quilting can blend in and leave your piecing and fabric to be the star, really stand out and add a whole new level of detail and design to your quilt, or fall somewhere between the two. Before jumping in, there are a few things to think about when planning your quilting:

- What level of design do you want to use? Something very intricate, or more straightforward?
- What type of design do you want to use? Edge to edge, echo, stitch in the ditch or custom?
- How do you want to do your quilting? By machine, hand or a combination of both?
- What role do you want your thread to play? Do you want it to stand out and really shine, or would you rather it blended in?

Quilting designs

Firstly, what is a quilting design? While quilt patterns (the instructions on how to make a quilt) are often referred to as quilt designs, in this context a quilting design is the line pattern created by stitching the quilt sandwich together. This can be something as simple as horizontal lines across the whole quilt or something more intricate with multiple layers of quilting and lots of detail.

Layers in a quilting design refer to the number of passes you need to make over the quilt to create the final look you want to achieve. For example, a grid is a two-layer design as you need to pass over the quilt twice to create the finished grid. If you need to make three passes, such as in a divided diamond design, then you are quilting a three-layer design and so on.

An example of a one-layer quilting design using a decorative machine stitch.

An example of a four-layer quilting design using straight lines.

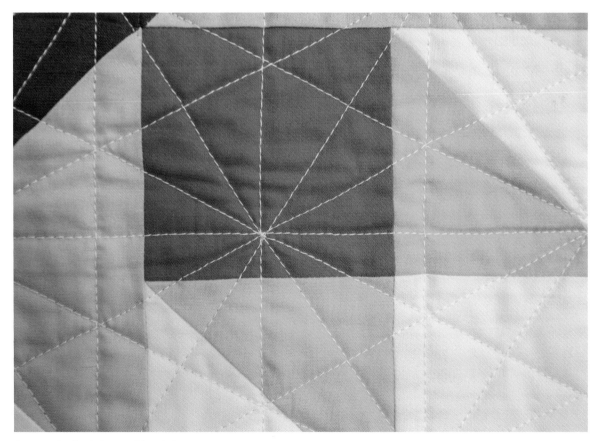

An example of a six-layer quilting design.

Example of a two-layer design

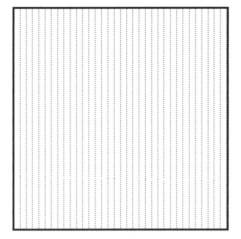

Layer 1 – vertical.

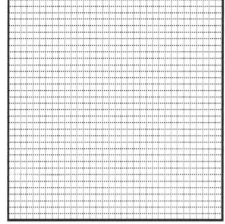

Layer 2 – horizontal.

Example of a three-layer design

Layer 1 – right diagonal.

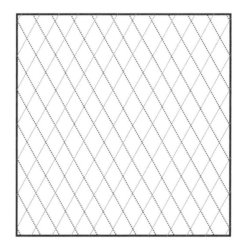

Layer 2 – left diagonal.

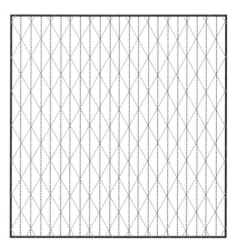

Layer 3 – vertical.

How to choose a quilting design

It is very easy to be caught in decision paralysis when it comes to choosing a quilting design for fear of 'ruining' your quilt and wasting all your hard work. It is important to remember that there is no one perfect quilting design for a quilt – often many different options can look great, and what one quilter thinks is perfect may not match what another thinks (and often doesn't!). When it comes down to it, you should choose a design according to *your* preferences, and no-one else's.

Quilting designs can generally be categorised into four types:

- Edge-to-edge designs which allow you to sew continuously from one edge of a quilt to another without stopping, removing the need to bury threads.
- Echo designs which are formed from lines that follow the edge of a shape and echo out like ripples in a pond.

Edge-to-edge quilting.

An example of an edge-to-edge design.

Echo quilting.

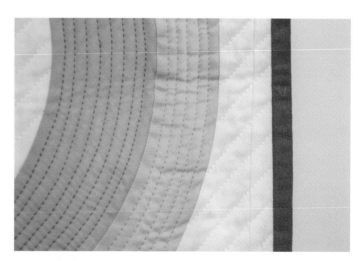

An example of an echo design.

Custom quilting.

- Stitch-in-the-ditch quilting which involves sewing within (or a thread's width to one side of) the seam lines of your quilt top to hide the quilting stitches.
- Custom designs which are adapted to the shapes and piecing in your individual quilt top to emphasise and complement different shapes in different ways.

An example of a custom quilting design.

While sometimes you will look at a quilt top and instantly know exactly how you want to quilt it, it usually takes a little more thought to find the option that feels best to you. Some things to bear in mind when choosing a design:

- Quilting designs show up more with thicker threads and on solid fabrics and less with thinner threads and on detailed prints.
- Dense quilting reduces the loft of your batting and gives the quilt a more structured feeling while more spaced-out quilting maintains the loft and gives a softer feel. Remember to check your batting for the maximum recommended distance between quilting lines.
- Edge-to-edge designs are usually quicker than custom quilting.
- Large quilts can be difficult to manoeuvre through a small sewing machine throat space so may not be as well suited to intricate quilting designs as a smaller quilt.

If you still find yourself stuck, try using the following prompts to help guide you:

- Do you want to subtly complement your piecing?
- Do you want the quilting to blend in?
- Do you need to finish the quilt quickly to meet a deadline?
- Do you want the quilting to take a starring role?
- Do you want to complement or contrast any patterned fabric used?
- Do you want a dense and structured-feeling quilt or a softer and looser quilt?

Marking your quilting design
Once you have chosen your quilting design, unless you are using your seams as a guide, you will likely need to mark up your quilt ready to start sewing. Marking up a quilt is the process of temporarily marking your quilting lines to act as a guide when quilting to help keep everything neat and in line.

Working one layer at a time and using your preferred removable fabric marker or Hera marker (*see* Chapter 3 for a discussion of the benefits of each type), simply draw the line you wish to quilt exactly where you wish to quilt it.

When marking straight lines, a quilting rule is invaluable: simply use the inch and angle degree lines to help you accurately mark your lines at precise intervals and angles. To mark more complicated designs, quilting stencils are a great option. Usually made from a thin acetate with the design cut out so you can mark the design on your quilt top easily, stencils can be especially helpful for more intricate curved and hand-quilting designs.

Machine quilting
The most popular method of quilting, machine quilting can be divided into two broad categories: long arm quilting and domestic quilting. Within the umbrella of domestic quilting there are also two sub-categories: walking-foot quilting and free-motion quilting (also referred to as FMQ). Whichever method you choose to use, thread quality is important, and you should always use a good-quality thread to avoid snagging, fraying and other problems down the line.

Long arm quilting
Long arm quilting uses a specialist quilting machine consisting of a sewing machine head and large frame that can be guided either by a computerised programme or manually. In both methods the long arm machine is moved over the quilt rather than the quilt being moved under the machine. Due to the highly specialised nature, large size and expensive cost of these machines, most quilters do not own one. It is often possible to rent time on a long arm machine, with the initial session usually including an overview of the technique and basic machine maintenance.

If you do not want to quilt your finished quilt yourself, perhaps because it is too big to easily manage with your domestic machine, you want a complex design, or maybe you just prefer not to quilt it yourself, it is possible to send quilt tops to long arm quilters to have them professionally quilted. Prices are often based on the square inch size of the finished quilt and whether the quilting design will be stitched from a computerised pantograph (a continuous line edge-to-edge quilting design that covers the entire quilt top), a hand-guided pantograph, or with fully or partially custom hand-guided quilting, and can become quite expensive.

When you want to highlight complex piecing, sometimes a simple grid is the best option.

Mixing different thread colours can have a striking visual impact across different coloured fabrics.

Simple lines combined with echo quilting can create a beautiful balance between structured and freer quilting styles.

Free-motion quilting

Free-motion quilting is the technique of quilting with lowered feed dogs so that you can move the quilt freely in all directions and control stitch length yourself. Ideal for intricate drawn designs that minimise the need to rotate your quilt through the throat space, it is possible to quilt any shape imaginable using this technique. Full details on how to free-motion quilt will not be covered here in favour of the more beginner-friendly walking-foot method.

Walking-foot quilting

Also known as an even feed or dual feed foot, a walking foot is a specialist presser foot for domestic machines that provides a second set of feed dogs to help feed the multiple layers of a quilt through your machine at an even rate and without slippage between layers. Walking-foot quilting refers to any quilting where you use this foot and is well suited to all four types of quilting design as discussed above.

While the walking foot is best known for straight-line quilting designs that use only straight lines, including those that have turns and pivots, it is also capable of quilting gentle curves such as waves, organic lines, circles and spirals. It is also possible to use in conjunction with the decorative stitch options many sewing machines offer, which, when used as a quilting stitch, can add an extra-special touch to your quilt. A popular decorative stitch option is a curved stitch which gives the illusion of having quilted a squiggly line without having to manually guide the quilt to create a consistently neat and even squiggle. Small stars, loops, zig zags and more can all add a unique and interesting visual detail – just remember to test any potential stitches on a scrap sample and check what the back of the stitch looks like before starting to sew on your quilt.

Most walking feet come with a removable guide bar used to quilt at regular intervals without the need to mark every individual line – simply mark the first quilting line to use as registration line and work outwards from there. It is important to check the distance it is set at after each line as it is easy to knock it slightly out of alignment while moving the quilt through your machine. An ⅛in error won't seem like much initially, but by the time you've quilted eight lines you're a whole inch out and the overall impact of the quilting design may be negatively affected.

STEP-BY-STEP: HOW TO QUILT WITH A WALKING FOOT

Step 1: Set the stitch length between 2.4 and 3mm. Note that this is just a guide, and you should experiment with different thread weights and stitch lengths to discover which combinations you prefer.

Step 2: Turn down the speed – a walking foot is designed to walk, not run! If you struggle to control the speed with your foot pedal alone, turning down the maximum speed setting on your machine (not all machines will have this option) will help keep you at a steady pace.

Step 3: Start stitching in the middle of the quilt and work outwards to ensure any spreading is evenly distributed – this can be the literal middle of the quilt for any non-edge-to-edge design, or the middle of one side when quilting from one side to the other.

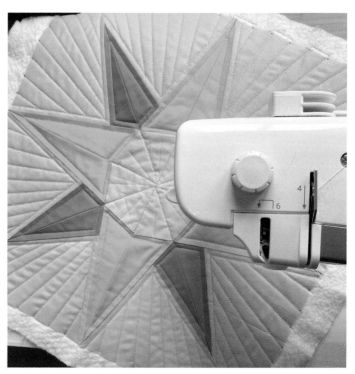

Walking foot quilting can create interesting and impactful designs using just straight lines.

Burying threads

If you start or stop a quilting line in the middle of a quilt, or you lose bobbin chicken (the act of trying to sew to the end of a seam or quilting line before the bobbin thread runs out), you will need to hide the loose thread ends. Burying threads is the process of securing and hiding these loose threads in the batting of your quilt and it is recommended that you bury your threads as you quilt to save yourself from a long session of thread burying at the end of quilting.

TOP TIP

Use easy threading or self-threading needles when burying threads to speed the process up.

When burying lots of threads at a time, a small dish to hold trimmed ends can help keep everything tidy as you work.

STEP-BY-STEP: HOW TO BURY THREADS

When starting quilting:

Step 1: Insert the needle at the start of your quilting line then pull up the bobbin thread to the top of the quilt by holding your top thread tail taut and manually moving the needle until a small loop of bobbin thread shows. Using a pin, stiletto point or tweezers, gently pull the loop so that the bobbin thread is on top of the quilt.

Step 2: Pull both threads so that you have a tail of approximately 5in and re-insert the needle at the start of your quilting line.

Step 3: Holding both threads taught, start quilting the line. Once you are a comfortable distance away from the starting point (generally around 12in or more), tie a small knot in the threads then thread a hand-sewing needle with both threads at once.

Step 4: Insert the needle at the beginning of your first stitch and instead of going all the way through the quilt sandwich, keep it in the batting layer and bring it up a few inches from the stitch, gently pull the knot through to finish the stitch and trim the tail so that no loose threads are showing.

When finishing quilting:

Step 1: When you are at the end of your quilting line, lift the needle and cut your threads so they are at least 5in long.

Step 2: Tie a small knot in the threads then thread a hand-sewing needle with one thread at a time.

Step 3: Insert the needle at the beginning of your last stitch and instead of going all the way through the quilt sandwich, keep it in the batting layer and bring it up a few inches from the stitch, gently pull the knot through to finish the stitch and trim the tail so that no loose threads are showing.

Hand quilting

Just as any quilt can look traditional or modern depending on the fabrics and colour placement, the final look of hand quilting can be as modern or traditional as you want depending on your thread colour, weight and stitch type. Just because it has a strong history and grounding in traditional quilts does not mean hand quilting should be overlooked when it comes to finishing a modern quilt and it has had a huge surge in popularity among modern quilters in recent years.

Finishing a quilt by hand has many positives:

- It gives you time to slow down and spend some quality time with your quilt.
- The repetitive motion can be an excellent mindfulness tool to help you be present in the moment.
- It's a simple and effective way to add lots of delicious texture to a quilt.
- Hand stitching lets you accent shapes and make the most of negative space without having to wrestle a large quilt through a small machine throat space.
- It can be done on the sofa while watching TV or listening to an audio book giving you the chance to snuggle under the quilt before it's even finished.

The possibilities of big stitch hand quilting are endless and can give your quilts some beautiful texture.

Using minimal machine quilting to give background structure, the hand quilting is the star of this quilt and really elevates the finished look.

Cushions are the ideal hand-quilting project where a small amount of stitching can have a big impact.

Thread

When you are hand quilting, your thread choice is going to have a big impact on the overall look of your quilt. The higher the weight number, the finer the thread and the smaller your stitches will need to be. If the fine and delicate stitches of the traditional hand-quilting style are your preference, head towards the 40 or 50wt threads. If you're after bolder and more modern stitches in the 'big stitch' style of hand quilting, you've got a few more options including 3, 5, 8 or 12wt threads or embroidery floss. Remember, just as if you were machine quilting, thread quality is important and you should always use a good-quality thread to avoid snagging, fraying and other problems.

Chapter 3 has a comprehensive guide walking you through the different thread weights and which needles to use, but there are some specific hand-quilting options worth thinking about:

- Pearl/Perlé cotton is a non-divisible thread with a lustrous sheen than comes in 3, 5, 8 and 12wt. The most used is the 8wt as this has a nice thickness and gives good definition without detracting too much from your piecing. The biggest brand for this type of thread is DMC and you can buy by the skein or the ball depending on how much thread you need.

- For Aurifil fans, their cotton 12wt is a non-divisible thread similar to perlé cotton. A little thinner than the 8wt perlé cotton, this thread still has a good definition and is great for adding that hand-sewn touch without overwhelming your quilt design.
- Embroidery floss is a less commonly used option but is also the one with the most flexibility. A six-stranded divisible thread, you can choose exactly how thick you want it to be and it has the benefit of allowing you to colour match across different areas if you want to mix and match thread thicknesses. DMC is the most popular high-quality brand of embroidery floss.

When cutting your thread, as a rule of thumb you should never cut a length longer than that of your thumb to the centre of your chest. This will help keep the thread at a manageable length and reduce the likelihood of it knotting or snagging as you sew.

Stitching

The most common stitch used for hand quilting is the running stitch. To do the running stitch, insert your needle from one side of your quilt to the other and 'run' the needle and thread up and down. You can either pull your needle all the way through the quilt sandwich with every stitch (good if you want very precise and small stitches) or 'rock' it by pushing it part way through the quilt and then moving the sharp point all the way through at the next stitch. Depending on your needle length and quilt thickness, you may be able to stack a few stitches at a time using the rocking method which results in faster stitching.

As with walking-foot quilting, you will want to start stitching in the middle of the quilt and work outwards to ensure any spreading is evenly distributed – either the literal middle of the quilt or the middle of one side when quilting from one side to the other.

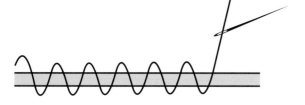

When making your stitches, aim for:

- Even spacing between stitches – ¼in is the most common but experiment to find a rhythm that works for you and the thickness of your thread.
- Regular stitch size – ⅛in to ¼in is the most common length as it is better for the structure of your quilt to have more small stitches than fewer large stitches. Smaller stitches are also less likely to snag when the quilt is used by pets and children and ruin your hard work.

When you first start hand quilting you might notice that the stitches on the back of your quilt aren't as even as the front – don't worry, this happens to everyone. Try adjusting the angle of the needle as it goes through the quilt sandwich and keep practising – it will get easier the more you do it.

Don't feel restricted to running stitch though – the world is your oyster! Any embroidery stitch can be used and often adds a whole new level to the texture of your quilt – French knots and seed stitch can give a quilt wonderful texture. However, some embroidery stitches can look messy on the back of the quilt so do be wary of what the back of the stitch looks like (unless it's a cushion cover or wall hanging where the back isn't going to be on show).

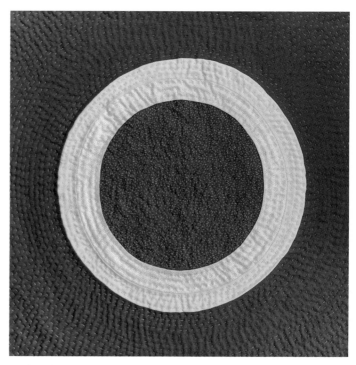

Seed stitch gives this quilt a beautiful texture and added visual interest.

STEP-BY-STEP: HIDING YOUR KNOTS

The easiest way to hide your knots is to insert the needle between the layers at the edge of your quilt within your binding allowance (usually ¼in to ½in), tuck the knot into the batting and trim the tail. However, this only works if you're able to use a single length of thread for the whole row. More often your quilt will be too wide, you'll want to change colour, or your thread will snap, and you will need to hide knots in the middle of a quilt.

To start in the middle of the quilt:

Step 1: Make a simple knot at the end of your thread and insert the needle between your quilt layers around ½in from where you want to start the first stitch and bring the point up at the point you want your first stitch to begin.

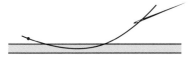

Step 2: Gently tug the knot through the top layer of fabric so that it pops into the batting layer. Don't worry if you accidentally pull it all the way through, just start again. If it's being a bit stubborn (more common with thicker threads), just keep gently tugging and easing the fabric around the thread until it's hidden.

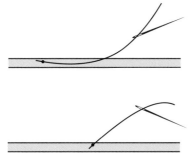

To finish in the middle of the quilt:

Step 1: Make a simple knot around ¼in (or just over your stitch length, whichever is longer) from the fabric before you insert the needle to make the final stitch.

Step 2: Insert the needle at the end of your final stitch and instead of going all the way through the quilt sandwich, keep it in the batting layer and bring it up at least 1in from the stitch, gently pull the knot through to finish the stitch and trim the tail.

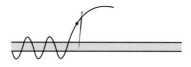

TRIMMING

Before you can bind and finish your quilt, it needs to be trimmed to remove excess backing and batting to prepare it for binding. Many quilts have square corners and so trimming is often referred to as squaring up, in other words ensuring that each corner is 90 degrees. Sharp corners are not the only option, however, with curved corners becoming increasingly popular.

While the odd sliver of batting peeking at the edge is fine, you want to make sure that no batting is showing within ¼in of the finished width of your binding. If you are trimming a very large quilt, or just want a very neatly trimmed quilt, consider using a removable fabric marker to mark the trimming lines before cutting.

BINDING

After quilting your quilt sandwich, it needs to be bound. Binding is a long strip of fabric which is sewn over the edges of a trimmed quilt as a border to hide and secure the raw edges and prevent fraying. The binding strip is attached to one side of the quilt before being wrapped around the edge to the other side and stitched down either by machine or hand.

Binding can be seen as the frame to your quilt, so consider which fabrics and colours will complement the top the most. A modern stripe? A solid colour matching the quilt top? A contrast colour to add a bit of pop? The possibilities are endless and there is no right answer – if you love it, it's perfect.

Generally made from quilting cotton, binding is cut either on the bias or the grain. Bias binding is cut on the bias to give it greater flexibility for curved or scalloped quilt edges. This can require more fabric and advance planning than non-bias (on the grain) binding, which is best suited to the straight edges and square corners found on most quilts and can be easily pieced from smaller pieces of fabric and left-over scraps.

As well as the fabric cut, binding can be broadly categorised in three ways: single-fold, double-fold and facing.

TOP TIP

If you work around the quilt rather than trimming opposite sides you are more likely to skew the angles of the corners to be greater than 90 degrees and need to trim more to make them square.

STEP-BY-STEP: HOW TO TRIM YOUR QUILT

Step 1: Using the longest ruler you have, start in the middle of a side and trim the excess off along the whole side. You may need to trim some of the quilt top due to slight shifting during the quilting process.

Step 3: Repeat with the remaining two sides. If squaring the quilt, ensure that the corners are at 90 degrees by aligning the edge of your ruler with the first trimmed edge before trimming the corner, while if you want curved corners, these can be easily trimmed using the edge of a plate or another appropriately sized curved object that you have to hand.

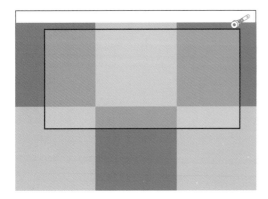

Step 2: Repeat step 1 on the opposite side of the quilt.

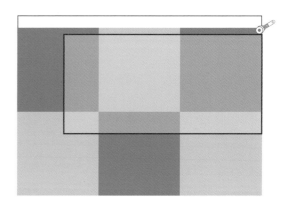

Varying binding colour and finishing method can add a fun and unique touch to your quilt and enhance the final finish.

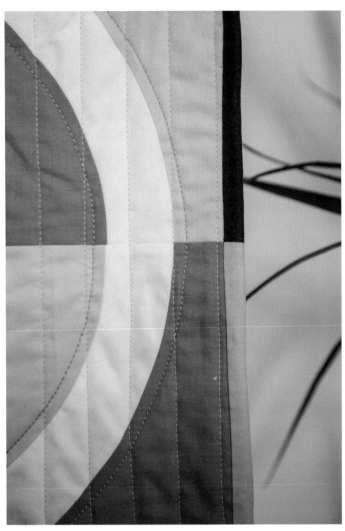

A pieced binding can add an extra design element to the finish of your quilt, here complementing the yellow quilting.

A blind-stitched binding gives a crisp and clean finish perfect for wall hangings or other display pieces.

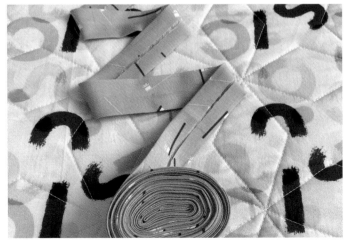

Using printed fabric for your binding can add a fun extra detail as well as tying it nicely to the quilt.

Single- and double-fold binding

Contrary to their names, single- and double-fold binding are not named for how many folds are pressed into the fabric before the binding is attached to your quilt but instead how many layers of fabric are folded over the edge of the quilt.

- Single-fold binding: only one layer of fabric covers the edge of the quilt as the binding edges are pressed inwards before attaching.
- Double-fold binding: two layers of fabric cover the edge of the quilt as the binding is pressed in half before attaching.

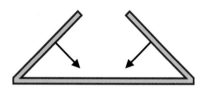 

Single-fold binding.   Double-fold binding.

Making binding

When making binding, the first question is how long is the total length of binding that you need? This is calculated by adding up the total perimeter of the quilt plus an allowance for seams and corners as follows:

2 × (length of quilt in + width of quilt in) + 20in = length of binding in

The second question to be answered is the width of binding to be cut for your desired finished width. The finished width of binding is the distance from the edge of the quilt to one edge of the binding, for example ½in. Calculate the binding width as follows:

SINGLE-FOLD BINDING:

- Finished width of binding in × 4 + ⅛in = cut binding width in
  - For example, a ½in finished binding would need to be cut at 2⅛in wide.

DOUBLE-FOLD BINDING:

- Finished width of binding in × 6 + ¼in = cut binding width in
  - For example, a ½in finished binding would need to be cut at 2¾in wide.

Once you know the length and width of binding needed, you can then cut and join your binding according to whether you are making bias or non-bias binding.

Scrappy binding is a great way to use up off-cuts of fabric and leftovers from a project to give a fun and unique finish to your quilt. To make your own scrappy binding, cut strips of any length in the desired width and join, repeating until you have the required length of binding.

NON-BIAS BINDING

Non-bias binding is made from strips cut on the grain which are then joined to form one long strip. While strips can be joined with a straight seam (where the short ends are joined end to end with a ¼in seam), an angled seam is generally recommended as this reduces bulk when folding the binding over.

To calculate how many strips you need, divide the length of binding needed by the width of fabric being cut:

$$\frac{\text{Length of binding in}}{\text{Width of fabric being cut}} = \text{number of strips}$$

CONTINUOUS BIAS BINDING

Bias binding can be made in the same way as non-bias binding, substituting strips cut on the grain for strips cut on the bias, however this can lead to stretched seams due to overhandling of bias edges. Instead, continuous bias binding is a quick and easy way to produce large quantities of bias binding with minimal sewing.

Continuous bias binding starts with a square which is then cut and sewn into a loop for easy cutting into a long strip. To calculate the starting square size you need, divide the length of binding needed by the width of fabric being cut and then find the square root:

$$\sqrt{\text{Length of binding} \times \text{width of binding}} = \text{size of starting square}$$

Backstitch at the beginning and end when joining strips to strengthen the seam.

STEP-BY-STEP:
HOW TO MAKE NON-BIAS BINDING

Step 1: Cut the required number of strips in the desired width.

Step 2: Placing two strips right sides together, join with a 45-degree seam across the corner as shown. Trim to ¼in seam and press open.

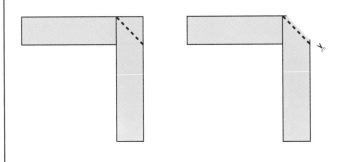

Step 3: Repeat to make a continuous length of binding.

Pressing binding

Once you have made your binding (regardless of the method), you need to press it in the style you wish to use, single- or double-fold.

Single-fold binding needs each long edge pressing in towards the middle of the wrong side of the bind strip, leaving a ⅛in gap in the centre. While this can be done by pinching the fabric in position while ironing close to your fingers, this risks burning your fingers. Instead consider buying a bias tape maker (this can be used for non-bias binding as well) to help protect your fingers and give a more precise press.

Double-fold binding is pressed by simply folding the binding strip in half lengthways and wrong sides together.

STEP-BY-STEP:
HOW TO MAKE CONTINUOUS BIAS BINDING

Step 1: Cut your starting square in half to produce two large triangles cut on the bias.

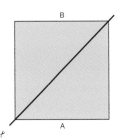

Step 2: Join the triangles to make a parallelogram.

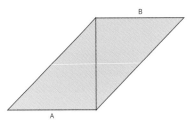

Step 3: Join the angled edges together to make a loop/tube, offsetting by the width of one strip (otherwise you'll make lots of loops rather than one long strip).

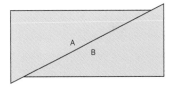

Step 4: Working in from one edge, cut at intervals the size of the required binding width.

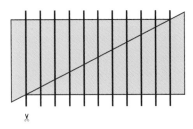

Attaching binding

Most quilters attach their binding by machine even if they plan to hand-finish it as it strengthens the edge of the quilt as well as saving time. To get the best results, a walking foot with a 90/14 quilting needle and 40–50wt piecing thread are recommended.

TOP TIP

If you struggle to feed the binding through a bias tape measure to start pressing, use the point of a pin to guide it through – usually two or three pin pushes is enough to get the fabric feeding through smoothly.

STEP-BY-STEP: ATTACHING TO THE QUILT AND SEWING MITRED CORNERS

Depending on how you wish to finish your binding, you will need to decide whether to attach it to the front or the back of your quilt. For machine finishes, typically binding is attached to the back to give greater control over the finished look of the front of the quilt. For hand finishes, binding is usually attached to the front to give a crisp front finish and hide any messy hand stitches, although if you want your hand stitches to be more of a feature, you can attach to the back.

Step 1: Starting at least 8–10in from a corner and leaving a loose tail of at least 6in, line up the edge of your binding with the edge of the quilt.
- Single-fold binding: Unfold one folded edge and line the raw edge up with the edge of the quilt, right sides together.
- Double-fold binding: Line up the raw edges of the binding with the quilt with the folded edge towards the centre of the quilt.

Step 2: Making sure to leave a loose tail of binding, start stitching the binding to the quilt using a 1.8–2.4mm stitch length.
- Single-fold binding: Use the crease line as a guide for where to sew.
- Double-fold binding: Sew the finished binding width distance in from the edge. For example, a ½in finished binding width should be sewn ½in from the edge of the quilt.

Step 3: Continue stitching until you are the finished binding width from the corner of the quilt then backstitch and cut your threads. For example, you should sew to ½in from the corner for a ½in finished binding width.

Step 4: Turning the quilt 90 degrees so that the next quilt edge is running towards you, fold the binding upwards at a 90-degree angle and then back down towards you so that the binding lies nice and flat and creates a sharp mitred corner turn.

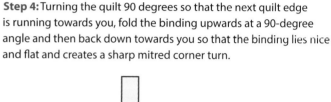

Step 5: Continue stitching along the edges of the quilt and turning at the corners as above until you are at least 6in from the point you started stitching your binding on, then backstitch and cut your threads. You should have at least a 6in tail of binding left from both the beginning and the end of the binding.

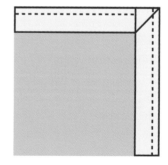

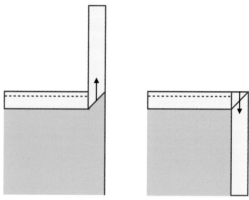

While not technically seamless, a so-called seamless join replicates the angled join of joining cut binding strips together to reduce bulk and hide the end point more cleanly (hence the name 'seamless').

Step 1: Using a removable marker, make a mark at the approximate halfway point between the beginning and end of your sewn binding. Mirror this mark on both binding tails so that when they overlap the mark is in the same place.

Step 2: Unfolding the ends of each binding tail, draw a line across the full binding width on either side of the initial mark so that the distance between them is the cut width of your binding. For example, if the cut width of binding is 2⅛in, the lines should be 1¹⁄₁₆in on either side as shown.

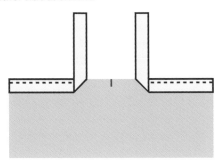

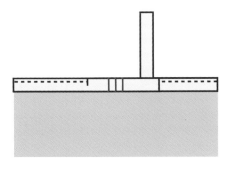

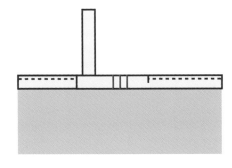

Step 3: Laying the binding tails over each other, cut each one at the line closest to the end of the tail so that when they are laid down, they overlap for exactly the cut width of your binding.

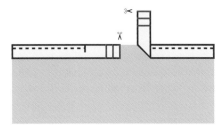

Step 4: Placing the cut ends right side together and matching the drawn lines into a square, join the strips in the same way as you join cut binding strips to make one long length of binding. You will need to scrunch the quilt up slightly to allow you to manoeuvre the join through your machine, and it is worth using pins to hold the ends in place to prevent slippage and an inaccurate seam.

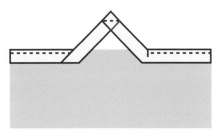

Step 5: Trim the seam allowance to ¼in and press open. Your binding should now lay flat against the quilt edge and all you need to do is sew over the unstitched gap, backstitching at the beginning and end to secure.

Bulkier than seamless joins, a straight end join gives a sharp 90-degree angle which can be helpful for accent binding section or occasions where you wish to match a binding seam to a particular seam or colour change in the quilt top.

Step 1: Using a removable marker, make a mark at the point you wish to make the binding seam. Mirror this mark on both binding tails so that when they overlap the mark is in the same place and extend it across the full binding width to show the stitching line.

Step 2: Unfolding the ends of each binding tail, draw a line across the full binding width approximately 1in on either side of the marked stitching line.

Step 3: Laying the binding tails over each other, cut each one at the line closest to the end of the tail so that when they are laid down, they overlap by 2in.

Step 4: Placing the cut ends right side together, join the strips by sewing along the stitching line. You will need to scrunch the quilt up slightly to allow you to manoeuvre the join through your machine, and you may want to use pins to hold the ends neatly in place.

Step 5: Trim the seam allowance to ¼in and press open. Your binding should now lay flat against the quilt edge. Sew over the unstitched gap, backstitching at the beginning and end to secure.

TOP TIP

Use a binding clip to hold the corner folds in place. This will lightly pre-press the fold and help hold everything in place while sewing the corner.

Finishing binding

Once your binding has been attached to one side of your quilt, it needs folding over and sewing down on the other side. This can be done either by machine or by hand depending on the finished look you wish to achieve, how quickly the quilt needs to be bound, and whether you enjoy hand stitching.

For both methods you will need to hold the folded-over binding in position while you stitch. Binding clips (also known by the brand name Wonder Clips) are small plastic clips used to hold the layers in place while moving the quilt through your machine or hand stitching in place. They are removed as you sew so you can easily clip smaller sections at a time and move them along rather than clipping the entire binding in place in one go.

When it comes to folding the corner fabric over you will notice that due to the neatly angled corner on the other side, you now have a slight excess of fabric. To make a matching neat corner, tuck in one side of corner fabric and fold the other side over the top to give a 45-degree angle.

When hand-stitching binding down, binding clips are a very helpful tool for keeping everything smoothly in place.

MACHINE FINISHING

Finishing binding by machine is a nice and fast way to sew your binding down, although it does take a little practice to get a neat and even stitch all the way around. The process is simple: fold over the binding and stitch a continuous line around the quilt at the edge of the binding.

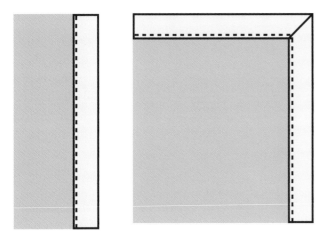

As when attaching the binding, a walking foot with a 90/14 quilting needle is recommended. The thread weight does not need to be limited to 40–50wt options however, and depending on how much of an impact you want your stitching to have, a thicker 28wt or even 12wt thread could be a good option. A stitch length of 2.4–3mm generally offers a nice balance with the thickness of binding, but you should experiment and see which you like most.

Machine binding does not need to be limited to a simple straight stitch, and the decorative stitches offered by many sewing machines can add an extra-special touch – just remember to test it out and check what the back of the stitch looks like before starting on your quilt.

HAND FINISHING

In comparison to machine finishing, hand stitching binding down is a much slower task, yet it often produces beautiful results that more than make up for the slower pace. There are two main stitches used to sew binding down by hand: big stitch binding and blind stitch binding. However, any hand sewing stitch should do the job.

Big stitch binding has seen a huge boom in popularity over recent years and is simply the process of using the big stitch hand-quilting technique with a heavy thread to give your binding a decorative finish.

For a more seamless finish, a blind stitch is the best option. For the most invisible finish use a medium- to light-weight thread that is colour matched to your binding and an appropriately sized needle. Start by hiding your knot in the binding allowance, then catch a few threads at a time of the quilt top before moving the needle into the fold of the binding for between ⅛in and ¼in. Next you will bring the needle out of the binding to catch a few threads of the quilt top, repeating all the way around the quilt.

Facing

Faced binding is a method of binding that gives a quilt a crisp edge with no visual border by turning the edge to the back of the quilt. Popular for art quilts, wall hangings and other display pieces, facing a quilt offers a smooth and highly professional-looking finish.

As when making binding, you will need to know the width of facing to be cut for your desired finished width. The finished width of facing is the distance from the edge of the quilt to one edge of the facing, for example 2in. Calculate the facing width as follows:

Finished width of facing + ¾in = cut facing width

Step 1: Cut four facing strips:
- Two strips the width of the quilt.
- Two strips the length of the quilt plus 2in.

Step 2: Fold ½in of fabric over wrong sides together along one long side of each cut strip and press.

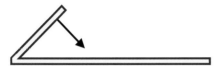

Step 3: Using a ¼in seam and right sides together, attach the raw edge of width of quilt pressed strips along both width of quilt edges. Sew from edge to edge.

Step 4: Fold back the attached strips and press outwards.

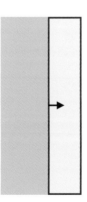

Step 5: Stitch in the ditch (some sewing machines come with a specific presser foot to help with accuracy). Stitch just to the right of the pressed seam to hold the attached facing strip in place.

Step 6: Fold the facing and ¼in seam over to the back of the quilt and press in place. The sewn stitch in the ditch line should be just rolling on the edge of the quilt.

Step 7: Hand stitch the facing in place using either a big stitch or blind stitch (*see* Finishing Binding above for more on these stitches).

Step 8: Repeat the process of attaching the facing strips from steps 3–6 using the length of quilt strips, ensuring that there is a 1in tail of binding at each end.

Step 9: Fold under the loose tails and press in place. Hand stitch the facing in place using either a big stitch or blind stitch, ensuring that you secure the tucked-in tails along the edge of the quilt.

HANGING SLEEVES

Many quilts go straight from sewing machine to being curled up underneath, but some quilts will need hanging sleeves attaching. If you want to hang a quilt in your home or enter a quilt into a show or competition, it will need a hanging sleeve attached to allow it to be displayed.

As with picking a backing and binding fabric, you will want to think about which fabric to use for your hanging sleeve. While they will not be on show, most quilters opt for something that matches the backing fabric, whether the same fabric or a co-ordinating solid. However, if the hanging sleeve is only temporary and will later be removed (for example, for display at a quilt show before being used at home), it may not be worth using the 'good' fabric and almost anything will suffice.

The width of a hanging sleeve will depend on the intended display: for quilt shows, hanging sleeves usually need to be at least 4in wide when attached, while for home display they only need to be approximately 1in wider than the hanging pole you will be using.

STEP-BY-STEP: HOW TO MAKE A HANGING SLEEVE

Step 1: Cut a long rectangle of fabric, the width of your quilt long by the required width:

- For a quilt show hanging sleeve, cut the fabric 10in wide.
- For a home display hanging sleeve, cut the fabric at least 3in wider than the hanging pole being used. For example, a 1in-wide pole would need the sleeve to be cut at least 4in wide.

Step 2: Fold over the short ends by an inch, press, then fold another inch and press again. Stitch in place with a row of stitching ¾in from the folded edge.

Step 3: With right sides together, align the long edge of the hanging sleeve and sew into a tube using a ¼in seam.

Step 4: Turn the hanging sleeve right sides out and press two creases along the length of the sleeve, ensuring to leave some ease to allow for the hanging pole to pass through.

Step 5: Pinning the hanging sleeve approximately 2in below the top edge of your quilt and centred, sew it to the back of your quilt. To avoid the stitching showing on the front of the quilt, a blind stitch finish is typically used (*see* Finishing Binding for more detail on this stitch).

TOP TIP

If your quilt is longer than your WOF, piece rectangles together using a ½in seam pressed open to make up the required length.

CHAPTER 7

THE QUILTS

Now that you've learned all about how to make and finish a quilt, it's time to put those new-found skills into practice. This chapter contains 11 quilt patterns (including a little bonus quilt made from some leftover blocks) which give you the chance to practise all the skills and techniques covered in this book.

Each pattern gives a full list of the materials needed, finished quilt and block measurements, a list of the techniques/blocks used, step-by-step piecing and finishing instructions, and an optional guide on how to quilt your finished quilt top in the same style as the sample quilt.

Fabrics used in quilt samples:

Bella White	Kona Lake	Kona Azure	Kona Pool	Kona Capri	Kona Breakers
Kona Turquoise	Kona Oasis	Kona Pacific	Kona Riviera	Kona Celestial	Kona Nightfall
Kona Lemon	Kona Sunny	Kona School Bus	Kona Torch	Kona Tangerine	Kona Pomegranate
Kona Salmon	Kona Peach	Kona Petal	Kona Wisteria	Kona Magenta	

MODERN SAMPLER

Many quilters start their quilting journey by making a sampler quilt and this book is no exception – with a modern twist on the classic style of course! Every block included in the Modern Sampler refers to the full instructions in Chapter 5, so if you have already made all 20 of the starred blocks from Chapter 5, you've almost made this quilt and just need to add sashing.

You will need

Fabric A (also used for sashing): 1 yard/metre
Fabric B: ⅝ yard/metre
Fabric C: ½ yard/metre
Fabric D: ¼ yard/metre
Fabric E: ¼ yard/metre
Binding: ¼ yard/metre
Backing: 1½ yards OR 1⅜ metres
Batting: 40 × 48in
One copy of Triangle block template
One copy of Quarter Circle templates A and B

One copy of Orange Peel templates A and B
Fabrics used in sample: Bella Solids White Bleached (A), Kona Turquoise (B), Kona Pacific (C), Kona Nightfall (D), Kona Sunny (E)

Finished measurements

Quilt: 34 × 42in
Blocks: 6 × 6in

Techniques/blocks used

Twenty different sample blocks from Chapter 5; sashing

CUTTING

Cutting for individual blocks is given with the instructions in Chapter 3, but if you prefer to cut everything at once you will need the following:

Step 1: From fabric A cut:
- Ten WOF × 2½in strips and sub-cut:
  - Twenty-five 2½ × 6½in rectangles
  - Six 2½ × 34½in strips of fabric A (sashing)
  - Two 1½ × 3½in rectangles
  - Two 1½ × 4½in rectangles
- One WOF × 8in strip and sub-cut:
  - One 8 × 8in square
  - Three ½ × 7½in squares
  - Two 3⅞ × 3⅞in squares (cut in half diagonally)
  - Two 3½ × 3½in squares
  - Two 2¾ × 2¾in squares
  - One 2½ × 2½in square

Step 2: From fabric B cut:
- One WOF × 8in strip and sub-cut:
  - One 8 × 4in rectangle
  - Three 7½ × 7½in squares
  - One 6½ × 3½in rectangle
  - Two 3 × 3in squares (cut in half diagonally)
  - Two 1½ × 6½in rectangles

- One 1½ × 3½in rectangle
- One 1½ × 2½in rectangle
- One WOF × 7in strip and sub-cut:
  - One 20 × 2½in rectangle
  - One 12 × 3½in rectangle
  - Three 7 × 7in squares
  - One 4 × 4in square
- One WOF × 5in strip and sub-cut:
  - One 5 × 5in square
  - One 4¾ × 4¾in square
  - Four 2¾ × 2¾in squares
  - Six 2½ × 2½in squares

Step 3: From fabric C cut:
- One 20 × 2½in rectangle
- One WOF × 7½in strip and sub-cut:
  - Four 7½ × 7½in squares
- One WOF × 7in strip and sub-cut:
  - One 7 × 7in square
  - One 6½ × 6½in square
  - One 4 × 4in square
  - Five 3½ × 3½in squares
  - One 2½ × 2½in square
  - One 1½ × 6½in rectangle
  - Four 1½ × 4½in rectangles
  - One 1½ × 3½in rectangle

Step 4: From fabric D cut:
- One WOF × 7½in strip and sub-cut:
  - One 20 × 2½in rectangle
  - One 7½ × 7½in square
  - One 4 × 4in square
  - One 3⅞ × 3⅞in square (cut in half diagonally)
  - Two 2¾ × 2¾in squares
  - One 1½ × 5½in rectangle
  - Two 1½ × 4½in rectangles
  - One 1½ × 2½in rectangle

Step 5: From fabric E cut:
- One WOF × 8in strip and sub-cut:
  - One 8 × 8in square
  - One 12 × 3½in rectangle
  - One 8 × 4in rectangle
  - One 7½ × 7½in square
  - One 6½ × 3½in rectangle
  - One 4 × 4in square
  - One 3⅞ × 3⅞in square (cut in half diagonally)
  - Two 3½ × 3½in squares
  - One 2¾ × 2¾in square
  - Eight 2½ × 2½in squares
  - One 1½ × 6½in rectangle
  - Three 1½ × 5½in rectangles
  - Two 1½ × 2½in rectangles

For each block, follow the instructions in Chapter 5.

Step 1: Make one Strip Piecing block.

Step 2: Make one Four-Patch block.

Step 3: Make one Nine-Patch block.

Step 4: Make one Disappearing Nine-Patch block.

Step 5: Make one Snowball block.

Step 6: Following the two-at-a-time method, make two Half-Square Triangles (HSTs). Repeat using one 4in square each of fabric C and E for a total of four HSTs. Join in a Four-Patch arrangement as shown.

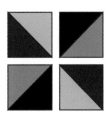 

Step 7: Make one four-colour Quarter-Square Triangle (QST).

Step 8: Make one three-colour QST.

Step 9: Make one two-colour QST.

Step 10: Make one split QST.

TOP TIP

To keep your blocks nice and straight when joining the rows together, use a removable fabric pen or chalk to mark where the blocks should line up as shown. Pin and sew together.

Step 11: Following the one-at-a-time method, make one Flying Geese block. Repeat using one 3½ × 6½in rectangle of fabric B and two 3½in squares of fabric A so that you have a total of two Flying Geese. Join as shown, pressing final seam open.

 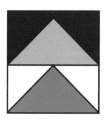

Step 12: Make two Half-Rectangle Triangles (HRTs) and join as shown. Press final seam open.

  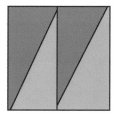

Step 13: Following the Triangle method, make one Square-in-a-Square (SIAS) block.

Step 14: Make one Double SIAS block.

Step 15: Make one Log Cabin block.

Step 16: Make one Quarter Log Cabin block.

Step 17: Make one Courthouse Steps block.

Step 18: Make one Triangles block.

Step 19: Make one Quarter Circle block.

Step 20: Make one Orange Peel block.

ASSEMBLY

Step 1: Using 2½ × 6½in rectangles of fabric A and pieced blocks, join rows in order shown. Press seams open.

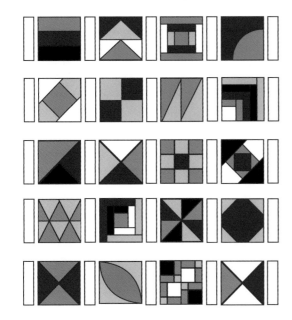

Step 2: Using 2½ × 34½in strips of fabric A, join rows as shown. Press seams open.

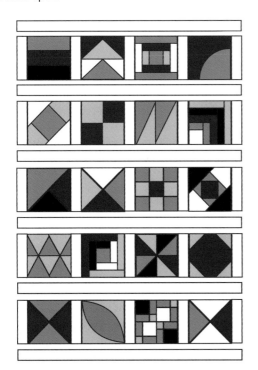

FINISHING

Step 1: Cut backing yardage to size. If you have directional fabric, you may need more than the given quantity of backing fabric.

Step 2: Baste and quilt as desired.

Step 3: Cut four WOF binding strips. Join and bind using preferred method.

HOW TO QUILT IT

The sample Modern Sampler was quilted using 40wt thread in a woven lattice design.

Step 1: Mark and quilt a 4in grid on a 45-degree angle across the quilt sandwich.

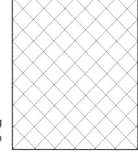

Step 2: Working across the quilted rows, mark and sew lines 1in apart as shown, taking care when stitching over the original grid lines to overlap your stitches.

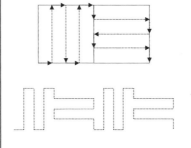

Step 3: Hand bind with big stitch binding and decorative cross stitches in the corners.

OCEAN CURRENTS

Ocean Currents makes the most of a gentle sea-inspired colour gradient with quick and easy strip-pieced blocks to give maximum impact. The large striped blocks pair perfectly with jumbo-sized Flying Geese, letting you show off those perfectly sharp points and create the illusion of the tide flowing in and out.

You will need
Fabric A: ⅝ yard/metre
Fabric B: ¼ yard/metre
Fabric C: ¼ yard/metre
Fabric D: ¼ yard/metre
Fabric E: ⅝ yard/metre
Fabric F: ⅜ yard/metre
Fabric G: ¼ yard/metre
Fabric H (background): 1⅛ yards/metres
Binding: ½ yard/metre
Backing: 2½ yards OR 2 ⅜ metres
Batting: 57 × 57in

Fabrics used in sample: Kona Azure (A), Kona Capri (B), Kona Pool (C), Kona Breakers (D), Kona Oasis (E), Kona Celestial (F), Kona Riviera (G), Bella Solids White Bleached (H)

Finished measurements
Quilt: 51 × 51in
Blocks: 9 × 9in

Techniques/blocks used
Strip Piecing, Flying Geese blocks; sashing

CUTTING

Step 1: Cut three WOF × 2in strips each of fabrics A, B, C, D, E and G, and two strips of fabric H.
Step 2: Cut one WOF × 2½in strip each of fabrics A, C and E.

Step 3: Cut one WOF × 10½in strips each of fabrics A and F and sub-cut three 10½ × 10½in squares of each fabric.

Step 4: Cut two WOF × 5½in strips each of fabrics E and H and sub-cut twelve 5½ × 5½in squares of each fabric.

Step 5: Cut 16 WOF × 1½in strips of fabric H. Sub-cut thirty 1½ × 9½in rectangles and reserve the remaining strips of fabric H.

TOP TIP

When adding your strips, work in alternating directions to minimise curving seams and keep your strips straight.

Strip Pieced block 1

Step 1 : Using WOF × 2in strips of fabrics A, B, C, D, E and G, piece in order along the long edge. Press seams open and repeat to make three strip sets.

Step 2: Cut your pieced panels into twelve 9½ × 9½in squares.

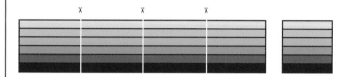

Strip Pieced block 2

Step 1: Take one WOF × 2½in strip each of fabrics A, C and E and two WOF × 2in strips of fabric H and piece in order along the long edge, pressing seams open.

Step 2: Cut your pieced panels into four 9½ × 9½in squares.

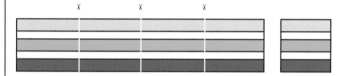

Flying Geese block 1

Step 1: Following the four-at-a-time Flying Geese method described in Chapter 5, use one 10½ × 10½in square of fabric A and four 5½ × 5½in squares of fabric E to make a set of four Flying Geese. Press seams to fabric E and trim to 5 × 9½in. Repeat to make a total of six Flying Geese (discard two as spares).

Step 2: Using one 10½ × 10½in square of fabric F and four 5½ × 5½in squares of fabric H, make a set of four Flying Geese. Press seams to fabric H and trim to 5 × 9½in. Repeat to make a total of six Flying Geese (discard two spare blocks).

Step 3: Join one of each Flying Goose blocks as shown, pressing seams upwards. Repeat to make six blocks.

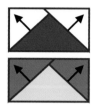

Flying Geese block 2

Step 1: Using one 10½ × 10½in square of fabric A and four 5½ × 5½in squares of fabric H, make a set of four Flying Geese. Press seams to fabric H and trim to 5 × 9½in. Discard one as spare.

Step 2: Using one 10½ × 10½in square of fabric F and four 5½ × 5½in squares of fabric E, make a set of four Flying Geese. Press seams to fabric E and trim to 5 × 9½in. Discard one as spare.

Step 3: Join one of each Flying Goose blocks as shown, pressing seams upwards. Repeat to make three blocks.

Sashing

Step 1: Join reserved 1½in strips of fabric H end-to-end to create one long strip. Sub-cut into six 1½ × 51½in rectangles.

TOP TIP

Sew the blocks together with the point of one showing on top to help you sew exactly across the tip to give a perfect sharp point to your Flying Geese.

ASSEMBLY

Step 1: Using 1½ × 9½in rectangles of fabric H and pieced blocks, join rows as shown. Press seams to fabric H.

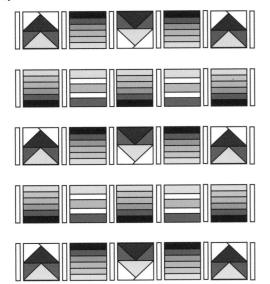

Step 2: Using 1½ × 51½in sashing strips, join rows as shown. Press seams to fabric H.

FINISHING

Step 1: Cut and piece backing yardage as shown below. If you have directional fabric, you will need more than the given quantity of backing fabric.

Note: All measurements show the size you should cut your backing fabric and *not* the finished measurements when pieces are joined.

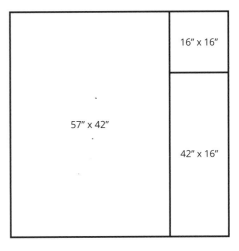

Step 2: Baste and quilt as desired.

Step 3: Cut six WOF binding strips. Join and bind using preferred method.

HOW TO QUILT IT

The Ocean Currents sample was quilted using 28wt thread in an intricate geometric design designed by Jacquie Gering called Diamonds in Diamonds from her book *Walk 2.0*. It was bound with a blind stitch finish.

TOP TIP

To keep your blocks nice and straight when joining the rows together, use a removable fabric pen or chalk to mark where the blocks should line up. Pin in place and sew together.

ROSE THORNS

This is a big quilt, there's no denying it, but don't get over-whelmed by the size. Extra-large Half-Rectangle Triangle blocks made in pairs mean this comes together much faster than you'd expect while helping you perfect your HRT trimming to create neat points. Paired with simple quilting and machine binding, Rose Thorns is a quick and satisfying make.

CUTTING

Step 1: Cut eight WOF × 7in strips of fabric A and sub-cut into twenty-four 7 × 14in rectangles.
Step 2: Cut nine WOF × 7in strips of fabric B and sub-cut into twenty-seven 7 × 14in rectangles.

Step 3: Cut four WOF × 7in strips of fabric C and sub-cut into ten 7 × 14in rectangles.

Step 4: Cut five WOF × 7in strips of fabric D and sub-cut into fourteen 7 × 14in rectangles.

TOP TIP

When piecing large blocks, use pins to stop your fabric from shifting while you sew.

ASSEMBLY

Step 1: Join three row As and three row Bs together, pressing the seams on each row in alternating directions as shown to help nest seams when joining rows together.

Step 2: Join rows together as shown. Press final joining seams open.

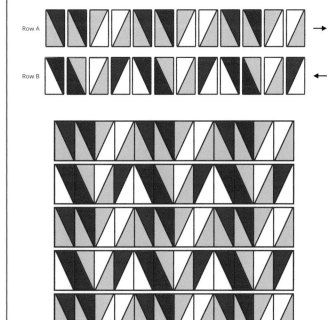

FINISHING

Step 1: Cut and piece backing yardage as shown. If you have directional fabric, you will need more than the given quantity of backing fabric.

Note: All measurements show the size you should cut your backing fabric and *not* the finished measurements when pieces are joined.

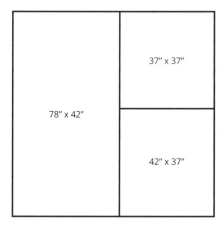

Step 2: Baste and quilt as desired.

Step 3: Cut eight WOF binding strips. Join and bind using preferred method.

HOW TO QUILT IT

The Rose Thorns sample was quilted using 40wt thread in a fun and simple wavy stitch design.

Step 1: Select a wavy stitch setting on your sewing machine and quilt vertical lines approximately 1½in apart.

Step 2: Machine bind using a decorative embroidery stitch.

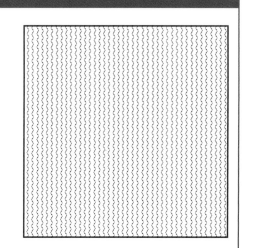

TOP TIP

Try different stitch widths and lengths on scrap fabric and batting before starting to sew to find your perfect squiggle.

Step 1: Following the Half-Rectangle Triangle method described in Chapter 5, use 7 × 14in rectangles of fabrics A and B to make two right-leaning HRTs. Press to fabric B and trim to 6½ × 12½in. Repeat to make a total of twenty-seven HRT As (discard one spare).

Step 2: Using 7 × 14in rectangles of fabrics A and C, make two right-leaning HRTs. Press to fabric C and trim to 6½ × 12½in. Repeat to make a total of nine HRT Bs (discard one spare).

Step 3: Using 7 × 14in rectangles of fabrics A and D, make two left-leaning HRTs. Press to fabric D and trim to 6½ × 12½in. Repeat to make a total of nine HRT Cs (discard one spare).

Step 4: Using 7 × 14in rectangles of fabrics B and C, make two left-leaning HRTs. Press to fabric C and trim to 6½ × 12½in. Repeat to make a total of nine HRT Ds (discard one spare).

Step 5: Using 7 × 14in rectangles of fabrics B and D, make two left-leaning HRTs. Press to fabric B and trim to 6½ × 12½in. Repeat to make a total of 18 HRT Es.

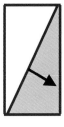

HRT A.

HRT B.

HRT C.

HRT D.

HRT E.

TOP TIP

Orientation of fabric and the diagonal sewing line is key here, so pay close attention when marking your guidelines and twisting your top rectangle.

CONSTELLATION

Quilters universally seem to love star quilts and this book wouldn't be complete without one, so here's the Constellation quilt! Using several simple building blocks to form two different styles of star, this design lends itself well to colour play to make it your own. Plus, the spare blocks from Star 1 can be used to make a bonus wall hanging, Trellis, giving you a cheeky two-for-one.

OVERVIEW

You will need
Fabric A (background): 2⅜ yards OR 2⅛ metres
Fabric B: ⅞ yard/metre
Fabric C: ½ yard/metre
Fabric D: ⅛ yard/metre
Fabric E: ⅛ yard/metre
Fabric F: ¼ yard/metre
Fabric G: ½ yard/metre
Fabric H: ¼ yard/metre
Fabric I: ¼ yard/metre
Binding: ½ yard/metre
Backing: 3 yards OR 2¾ metres
Batting: 62 × 62in

Fabrics used in sample: Bella Solids White Bleached (A), Kona School Bus (B), Kona Wisteria (C), Kona Lemon (D), Kona Pomegranate (E), Kona Magenta (F), Kona Petal (G), Kona Tangerine (H), Kona Sunny (I)

Finished measurements
Quilt: 56 × 56in
Blocks: 18 × 18in

Techniques/blocks used
Square-in-a-Square, Half-Square Triangles, Four-Patch blocks, Nine-Patch blocks, Three-Colour Quarter-Square Triangles, Split Quarter-Square Triangles; Sashing

CUTTING

Step 1: Cut one WOF × 8in strip each of fabrics A and I and sub-cut four 8 × 8in squares of each fabric.

Step 2: Cut three WOF × 7½in strips of fabric A and sub-cut fourteen 7½ × 7½in squares.

Step 3: Cut four WOF × 6½in strips of fabric A and sub-cut twenty 6½ × 6½in squares.

Step 4: Cut two WOF × 4 ¾in strips of fabric A and sub-cut nine 4¾ × 4¾in squares.

Step 5: Cut two WOF × 3½in strips each of fabrics A and H and sub-cut sixteen 3½ × 3½in squares of each fabric.

Step 6: Cut six WOF × 1½in strips of fabric A. Sub-cut six 1½ × 18½in rectangles and reserve the remaining strips of fabric A.

Step 7: Cut four WOF × 7in strips of fabric B and sub-cut twenty 7 × 7in squares.

Step 8: Cut two WOF × 7½in strips of fabric C and sub-cut ten 7½ × 7 ½in squares.

Step 9: Cut one WOF × 3⅞in strip of fabric D and sub-cut ten 3⅞ × 3⅞in squares. Cut squares in half diagonally to give 20 right-angled triangles of fabric D.

Step 10: Cut one WOF × 3⅞in strip of fabric E and sub-cut eight 3⅞ × 3⅞in squares. Cut squares in half diagonally to give 16 right-angled triangles of fabric E.

Step 11: Cut one WOF × 7½in strip of fabric F and sub-cut four 7½ × 7½in squares.

Step 12: Cut two WOF × 7½in strips of fabric G and sub-cut eight 7½ × 7½in squares.

Star 1

Step 1: Following the Single Square-in-a-Square Triangles method described in Chapter 5, use 4¾ × 4¾in square of fabric A and 3⅞in triangles of fabric D. Trim to 6½ × 6½in and repeat to make a total of five SIASs.

Step 2: Following the Split Quarter-Square Triangles method described in Chapter 5, use one 7½ × 7½in square each of fabrics A and C and one 7 × 7in square each of fabric B to make the blocks. Trim to 6½ × 6½in (the centre point for trimming is 3¼in) and repeat to make a total of 20 Split QSTs.

Note: This will produce 40 Split QSTs, of which only 20 will be the orientation required for this quilt. To save wasting the spare blocks, why not make the bonus Trellis quilt?

Step 3: Join sub-blocks and 6½ × 6½in squares of fabric A in a Nine-Patch construction as shown, pressing final seams open. Repeat to make five Star 1 blocks.

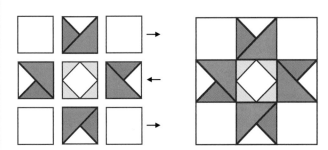

Star 2

Step 1: Following the Single SIAS Triangles method described in Chapter 5, use 4¾ × 4¾in square of fabric A and triangles of fabric E. Trim to 6½ × 6½in and repeat to make a total of four SIAS.

Step 2: Following the Three-Colour QST method described in Chapter 5, use 7½ × 7½in squares of fabric G and 7½ × 7½in square each of fabrics A and F to make blocks. Press to fabric G and final seam open. Trim to 6½ × 6½in (the centre point for trimming is 3¼in) and repeat to make a total of 16 Three-Colour QSTs.

Step 3: Following the eight-at-a-time Half-Square Triangles method described in Chapter 5, use 8 × 8in square each of fabrics A and I. Trim to 3½ × 3½in and repeat to make a total of 32 HSTs.

Step 4: Following the Four-Patch method described in Chapter 5, join two HSTs and one 3½ × 3½in square each of fabrics A and H. Repeat to make a total of 16 Four-Patches.

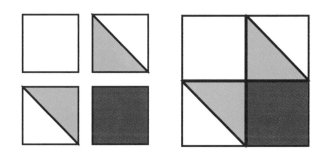

Step 5: Join sub-blocks in a Nine-Patch construction as shown. Repeat to make four Star 2 blocks.

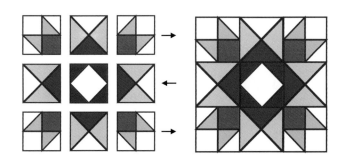

Step 1: Join reserved 1½in strips of fabric A end-to-end to create one long strip. Sub-cut into two 1½ × 56½in rectangles.

ASSEMBLY

Step 1: Using 1½ × 1½in rectangles of fabric A and pieced blocks, join rows as shown. Press seams to fabric A.

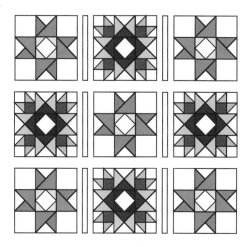

Step 2: Using 1½ × 56½in sashing strips, join rows as shown. Press seams to fabric A.

TOP TIP

To keep your blocks nice and straight when joining the rows together, use tailor's chalk or a removable fabric pen to mark where the blocks should line up as shown. Pin together and sew together.

FINISHING

Step 1: Cut and piece backing yardage as shown below. If you have directional fabric, you will need more than the given quantity of backing fabric.

Note: All measurements show the size you should cut your backing fabric and *not* the finished measurements when pieces are joined.

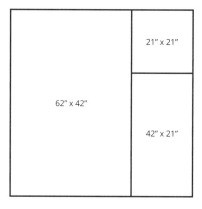

Step 2: Baste and quilt as desired.

Step 3: Cut six WOF binding strips. Join and bind using preferred method.

HOW TO QUILT IT

The Constellation sample was quilted using 40wt thread in an intricate geometric design designed by Jacquie Gering called The Six Set Grid from her book *Walk 2.0*. It was bound with a blind stitch finish.

TRELLIS

This quilt is a bonus quilt that can be whipped up in no time using just the left-over Split Quarter-Square Triangle blocks from the Constellation quilt – waste not, want not! Before joining the blocks together, take some time to play around with different block arrangements and orientations as the possibilities to make this quilt totally unique to you are almost endless.

OVERVIEW

You will need
Twenty discarded Split QST blocks from making the Constellation quilt
Binding: ¼ yard/metre
Backing: 1 yard/metre
Batting: 30 × 36in

Finished measurements
Quilt: 24 × 30in
Blocks: 6 × 6in

Techniques/blocks used
Split Quarter-Square Triangles

ASSEMBLY

Step 1: Using 20 spare Split QSTs from Constellation, join rows together, pressing the seams on each row in alternating directions as shown to help nest seams when joining rows together.

Step 2: Join rows together as shown. Press final joining seams open.

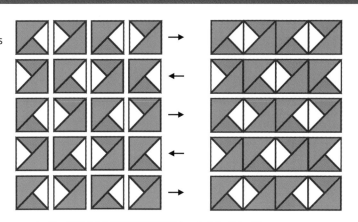

FINISHING

Step 1: Cut backing yardage to size.

Step 2: Baste and quilt as desired.

Step 3: Cut three WOF binding strips. Join and bind using preferred method.

The Trellis sample was quilted using both 40wt and 12wt thread in a combination of machine and hand quilting.

Step 1: With 40wt thread, mark and quilt lines 1in apart across the coloured lattice sections as shown.

Step 2: Hand quilt between the sewn 1in lines using 12wt thread.

Step 3: In the lattice gaps, hand quilt three concentric squares ½in apart as shown.

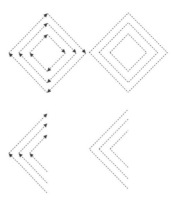

Step 4: Hand bind with a blind stitch.

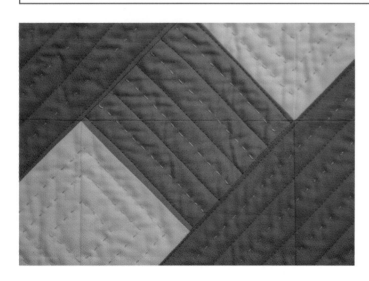

NEBULA

Nebula helps you step beyond the standard blocks used until now into more unusual piecing techniques for an advanced beginner/intermediate level design with a real modern 'wow' factor. Don't be intimidated by the need to cut some assembled blocks in half – just breathe, double check your ruler placement and go for it.

You will need
Fabric A (Background): 2 yards OR 1¾ metres
Fabric B: ⅜ yard/metre
Fabric C: ⅜ yard/metre
Fabric D: ⅛ yard/metre
Fabric E: ⅛ yard/metre
Fabric F: ¼ yard/metre
Fabric G: ⅜ yard/metre
Fabric H: ⅜ yard/metre
Binding: ½ yard/metre
Backing: 2⅜ yards OR 2¼ metres
Batting: 56 × 56in

Fabrics used in sample: Bella Solids White Bleached (A), Kona Tangerine (B), Kona Sunny (C), Kona Turquoise (D), Kona Pacific (E), Kona Nightfall (F), Kona Peach (G), Kona Salmon (H)

Finished measurements
Quilt: 49½ × 49½in
Blocks: 24 × 24in

Techniques/blocks used
Square-in-a-Square, Snowball Corners, Four-Patch blocks, Nine-Patch blocks

CUTTING

Step 1: Cut four WOF × 7½in strips of fabric A. Sub-cut sixteen 10½ × 7½in rectangles.

Step 2: Cut two WOF × 5in strips of fabric A. Sub-cut sixteen 5 × 5in.

Step 3: Cut one WOF × 5⅞in strip of fabric A. Sub-cut four 5⅞ × 5⅞in squares and four 5⅜ × 5⅜in squares.

Step 4: Cut three WOF × 3in strips of fabric A. Sub-cut thirty-two 3 × 3in squares.

Step 5: Cut four WOF × 1½in strips of fabric A. Sub-cut sixteen 1½ × 3⅜in rectangles and sixteen 1½ × 5⅜in rectangles.

Step 6: Cut five WOF × 1in strips of fabric A.

Step 7: Cut one WOF × 3in strip each of fabrics B, C, G and H. Sub-cut eight 5 × 3in rectangles of each fabric.

Step 8: Cut one 7 × 7in square each of fabrics B, C, G and H.

Step 9: Cut one WOF × 4⅜in strip each of fabrics D and E. Sub-cut eight 4⅜ × 4⅜in squares of each fabric. Cut squares in half diagonally to give 16 right-angled triangles each of fabrics D and E.

Step 10: Cut one WOF × 3⅜in strip of fabric F. Sub-cut eight 3⅜ × 3⅜in squares.

Step 11: Cut one WOF × 3in strip of fabric F. Sub-cut eight 3 × 3in squares.

Double Square-in-a-Square

Step 1: Following the Single SIAS Triangles method described in Chapter 5 and pressing seams open, use 5⅜ × 5⅜in square of fabric A and two 4⅜in triangles each of fabrics D and E, alternating triangle fabrics as shown. Trim to 7½ × 7½in and repeat to make a total of four Single SIAS.

Step 2: Join 4⅜in triangle of fabric D with 4⅜in triangle of fabric E as shown, pressing seams open. Repeat to make eight joined triangles.

Step 3: Following the Snowball Corners method described in Chapter 5, use 5⅞ × 5⅞in square of fabric A and two 3 × 3in squares of fabric F, snowballing opposite corners as shown. Press to fabric F and repeat to make a total of four snowballed sub-blocks.

Step 4: Cut Snowball blocks in half diagonally as shown.

Step 5: Using Single SIAS, triangle and cut Snowball blocks, assemble Double SIAS as shown, attaching Triangle blocks first. Repeat to make a total of four blocks.

continued on following page…

Corner block

Step 1: Following the eight-at-a-time Half-Square Triangle method described in Chapter 5, use 7 × 7in square each of fabrics B and C. Trim to 3 × 3in. Repeat with fabrics G and H.

Step 2: Following the Snowball Corners method described in Chapter 5 and pressing seams open, use 5 × 3in rectangle of fabric B and one 3 × 3in square of fabric A, snowballing one corner as shown. Repeat to make eight sub-blocks each of fabrics B, C, G and H, taking care to snowball the corner shown for each fabric.

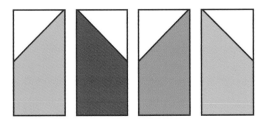

Step 3: Using one 5 × 5in square of fabric A, join sub-blocks together in a Four-Patch construction as shown, pressing the seams on each row in alternating directions as shown to help nest seams. Press final seam open and repeat to make eight fabric B/C and eight fabric G/H Corner blocks.

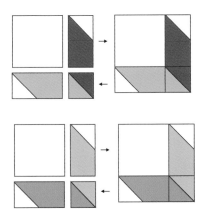

Inset Triangle block

Step 1: Following the Courthouse Steps method described in Chapter 5 and pressing seams open, use one 3⅜ × 3⅜in square of fabric F, two 1½ × 3⅜in rectangles and two 1½ × 5⅜in rectangles of fabric A as shown. Repeat to make eight sub-blocks.

Step 2 : Cut sub-blocks in half diagonally as shown and using a removable fabric marker, mark a line ¼in in from the cut edge on the reverse of the cut block.

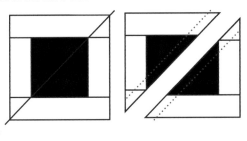

Step 3: Using 10½ × 7½in rectangle of fabric A and removable fabric marker, mark 5in out from one corner as shown.

Step 4: Right sides together, line up the marked line on cut sub-block with 5in marks and sew along the marked line. Trim excess corner fabric and dog ears and press seam open.

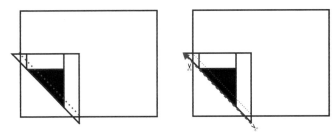

Step 5: Repeat steps 3 and 4 to make 16 Inset Triangle blocks, eight of each orientation.

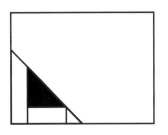

Orientation 1.

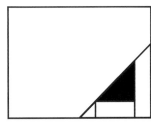

Orientation 2.

ASSEMBLY

Step 1: Join Double SIAS, Corner, and Inset Triangle blocks in a nine-patch construction as shown. Press seams on each row in alternating directions as shown to help nest seams when joining rows together. Repeat to make four blocks.

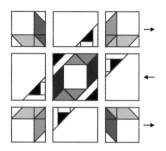

Step 2: Join blocks together in a Four-Patch construction as shown, pressing the seams on each row in alternating directions as shown to help nest seams when joining the quilt top together. Press final seam open.

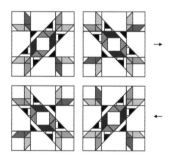

Border

Step 1: Join 1in strips of fabric A end-to-end to create one long strip. Sub-cut into two 1 × 48in rectangles and two 1 × 49½in strips.

Step 2: Attach 1 × 48in strips to opposite sides of the quilt top, pressing seams outward.

Step 3: Attach 1 × 49½in strips to opposite sides of the quilt top, pressing seams outward.

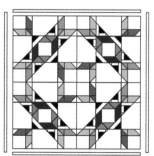

FINISHING

Step 1: Cut and piece backing yardage as shown below. If you have directional fabric, you will need more than the given quantity of backing fabric.

Note: All measurements show the size you should cut your backing fabric and *not* the finished measurements when pieces are joined.

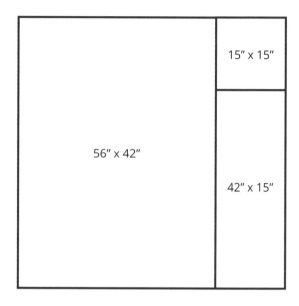

Step 2: Baste and quilt as desired.

Step 3: Cut six WOF binding strips. Join and bind using preferred method.

HOW TO QUILT IT?

The Nebula sample was quilted using 40wt thread in a simple diagonal grid design.

Step 1: Mark and quilt a 1in grid on a 45-degree angle across the quilt sandwich.

Step 2: Hand bind with big stitch binding.

SEA GLASS

Triangles hold a unique place in the quilting world as you get to skip the piecing stage and go straight from cutting to assembling the top – while slightly unconventional, it's great for a quick sense of accomplishment. Using big triangles in a row-style assembly, Sea Glass is great for practising precise point matching.

OVERVIEW

You will need
Fabric A: ½ yard/metre
Fabric B: ⅝ yard/metre
Fabric C: ¼ yard/metre
Fabric D: ½ yard/metre
Fabric E: ½ yard/metre
Fabric F: ¼ yard/metre
Fabric G: ¼ yard/metre
Binding: ¼ yard/metre
Backing: 1½ yards OR 1⅜ metres
Batting: 42 × 48in
One copy of Sea Glass template

Fabrics used in sample: Bella Solids White Bleached (A), Kona Azure (B), Kona Pool (C), Kona Breakers (D), Kona Oasis (E), Kona School Bus (F), Kona Pomegranate (G)

Finished measurements
Quilt: 36 × 42in

Techniques/blocks used
Triangle piecing

TOP TIPS

- When using a paper template, use a ruler to cover and protect the paper when cutting fabric.
- When cutting triangles rotate the template as shown, aligning sides to reduce waste and maximise triangles cut per strip.

CUTTING

Step 1: Cut two WOF × 6½in strips each of fabrics A and E and using Sea Glass template, sub-cut into 17 triangles of each fabric.

Step 2: Cut three WOF × 6½in strips of fabric B and using Sea Glass template, sub-cut into 23 triangles.

Step 3: Cut one WOF × 6½in strip of fabric C and using Sea Glass template, sub-cut into ten triangles.

Step 4: Cut two WOF × 6½in strips of fabric D and using Sea Glass template, sub-cut into 16 triangles.

Step 5: Cut one 18 × 6½in strip of fabric F and using Sea Glass template, sub-cut into four triangles.

Step 6: Cut one 18 × 6½in strip of fabric G and using Sea Glass template, sub-cut into four triangles.

ASSEMBLY

Step 1: With right sides together, form rows in order shown and pressing seams as shown before attaching the next triangle.

Step 2: With right sides together, join your rows along the long edge, taking care to nest seams. Press final seam open.

Step 3: Trim the quilt top to 36 × 42in as shown, discarding the trimmed edges.

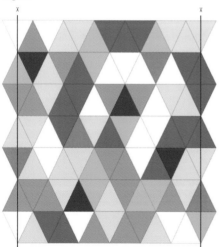

FINISHING

Step 1: Cut backing yardage to size.

Step 2: Baste and quilt as desired.

Step 3: Cut five WOF binding strips. Join and bind using preferred method.

HOW TO QUILT IT

The Sea Glass sample was quilted using 40wt thread in a design that echoes the piecing.

Step 1: Mark and quilt ½in lines within each coloured shape as desired. Try mixing up which direction each section goes in to add another layer of dimension to your quilt top.

Step 2: Hand bind with a blind stitch.

TOP TIPS

- Pay careful attention to the rotation and order of the triangles when piecing and make sure to line up the angled points from the template to help achieve precise points when joining rows together.

- Change thread colours across each fabric colour to add a beautifully luxurious finish to your quilt.

KOI POND

It's time to flaunt your curves with Koi Pond's bold Quarter Circle ring block. Surprisingly simple, the quarter rings are made in the same way as a standard Quarter Circle block, just doubled up. Curves don't need to be scary – just go slow, use pins when matching the seams and remember that every quilt is perfectly imperfect and not every ring has to be perfectly round to be perfect to you.

OVERVIEW

You will need
Fabric A: 1½ yards OR
  1⅜ metres
Fabric B: 1⅛ yards/metres
Fabric C: 1⅞ yards
  OR 1¾ metres
Fabric D: ⅝ yard/metre
Binding: ½ yard
Backing: 2¾ yards OR
  2⅝ metres
Batting: 60 × 60in
One copy of Koi Pond
  Outer template
One copy of Koi Pond
  Ring template
One copy of Koi Pond
  Inner template

Fabrics used in sample: Bella
  Solids White Bleached
  (A), Kona Lake¸ (B), Kona
  Turquoise (C), Kona
  Riviera (D)

Finished measurements
Quilt: 54 × 54in
Blocks: 9 × 9in

Techniques/blocks used
Curved piecing; Four-Patch
  construction, Nine-Patch
  construction

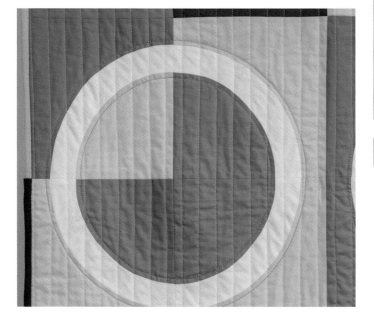

CUTTING

Step 1: Cut three WOF × 12in strips of fabric A, sub-cut 36 Koi Pond Ring template.

Step 2: Cut one WOF × 7in strip of fabric B, sub-cut four Koi Pond Inner template.

Step 3: Cut two WOF × 10¼in strips of fabric B, sub-cut 12 Koi Pond Outer template.

Step 4: Cut five WOF × 7in strips of fabric C, sub-cut 30 Koi Pond Inner template.

Step 5: Cut three WOF × 10¼in strips of fabric C, sub-cut 16 Koi Pond Outer template.

Step 6: Cut two WOF × 10¼in strips of fabric D, sub-cut eight Koi Pond Outer template.

Step 7: Cut two fabric D Koi Pond Inner template.

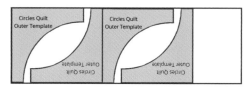
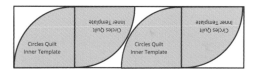
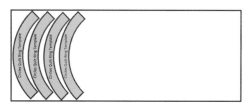

TOP TIP

Go slowly when sewing these blocks and take care not to stretch the rings when joining to help avoid puckers or an uneven quilt top.

Step 1: Following the Quarter Circle block method described in Chapter 5, use four fabric C Outers and fabric A Rings to make four sub-blocks as shown. Press seams open.

Step 2: Using four fabric B Inners and fabric C+A sub-blocks, make four Quarter Circle block 1s as shown. Trim to 9½ × 9½in using trimming guide as shown. Press seams open.

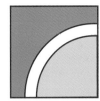

Quarter Circle block 1.

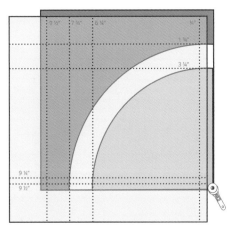

Trimming stage 1.

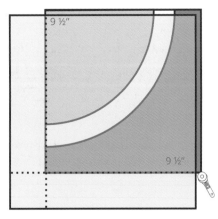

Trimming stage 2.

Step 3: Repeat using two fabric C Outers, fabric A Rings and fabric D Inners to make two Quarter Circle block 2s. Trim to 9½ × 9½in.

Quarter Circle block 2.

Step 4: Repeat using ten fabric C Outers, fabric A Rings and fabric C Inners to make ten Quarter Circle block 3s. Trim to 9½ × 9½in.

Quarter Circle block 3.

Step 5: Repeat using 12 fabric B Outers, fabric A Rings and fabric C Inners to make 12 Quarter Circle block 4s. Trim to 9½ × 9½in.

Quarter Circle block 4.

Step 6: Repeat using eight fabric D Outers, fabric A Rings and fabric C Inners to make eight Quarter Circle block 5s. Trim to 9½ × 9½in.

Quarter Circle block 5.

TOP TIP

Precision trimming is essential here to help achieve perfectly matched rings when assembling – take your time and be careful when cutting.

ASSEMBLY

Step 1: Join two Quarter Circle block 5s and two Quarter Circle block 3s in a Four-Patch arrangement as shown. Repeat to make four Circle 1 blocks.

Circle 1.

Step 2: Join three Quarter Circle block 4s and one Quarter Circle block 1 in a Four-Patch arrangement as shown. Repeat to make four Circle 2 blocks.

Circle 2.

TOP TIP

To ensure your rings match exactly to form a perfect circle, pin both sides of fabric A in place to prevent shifting.

Step 3: Join two Quarter Circle block 2s and two Quarter Circle block 3s in a Four-Patch arrangement as shown to make one Circle 3 block.

Circle 3.

Step 4: Join Circle blocks 1, 2 and 3 in a Nine-Patch construction as shown, pressing the seams on each row in alternating directions to help nest seams when joining rows together. Press final seams open.

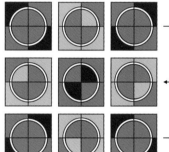

FINISHING

Step 1: Cut and piece backing yardage as shown below. If you have directional fabric, you will need more than the given quantity of backing fabric.

Note: All measurements show the size you should cut your backing fabric and *not* the finished measurements when pieces are joined.

Step 2: Baste and quilt as desired.

Step 3: Cut six WOF binding strips. Join and bind using preferred method.

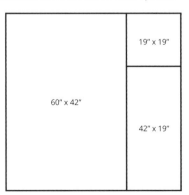

HOW TO QUILT IT

The Koi Pond sample was quilted using both 40wt and 12wt thread in a combination of straight-line and circular quilting.

Step 1: With 40wt thread, mark and quilt lines 1in apart vertically across the quilt sandwich.

Step 2: Using 12wt thread sew continuous circles ½in inside and outside each pieced ring.

Step 3: Piece accent binding and hand bind with big stitch binding.

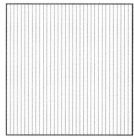

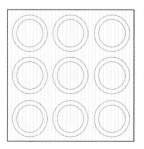

FLOWERS

Flowers is a celebration of how bold but simple piecing can create a big impact. It comes together super-fast thanks to big block curves and large triple inset circles and really lends itself to playful quilting details. For the perfect finishing touch, add hand-embroidered stamens to the flowers for that extra 'wow' factor.

You will need
Fabric A (background): 1⅛ yards/metres
Fabric B: ½ yard/metre
Fabric C: ½ yard/metre
Fabric D: ⅜ yard/metre
Fabric E: ⅜ yard/metre
Binding: ¼ yard/metre
Backing: 1½ yards/metres
Batting: 44 × 44in
One copy of Flowers template A
One copy of Flowers template B
One copy of Flowers template C
One copy of Flowers template D
One copy of Flowers template E
One copy of Flowers template F
One copy of Flowers template G
One copy of Flowers template H

Fabrics used in sample: Bella Solids White Bleached (A), Kona Pool (B), Kona Breakers (C), Kona Pomegranate (D), Kona Torch (E)

Finished measurements
Quilt: 38 × 38in
Blocks: 9 × 9in (Quarter Circles), 18 × 18in (Inset Circles)

Techniques/blocks used
Inset Circles, Curved Piecing, Four-Patch blocks; Four-Patch construction

CUTTING

Step 1: Cut one WOF × 18½in strip of fabric A, sub-cut two 18½in squares. Fold your squares into quarters and cut two Flowers template A, taking care to align the corner of the template with the folded corner of your fabric as shown. Fold circles into quarters and cut two Flowers template F. Keep outer squares and inner circles, discarding rings.

Step 2: Cut eight Flowers template G of fabric A.

Step 3: Cut four WOF × 1¼in strips of fabric A. Sub-cut into two 1¼ × 36½in strips and two 1¼ × 38½in strips.

Step 4: Cut one WOF × 17½in strip of fabric B, sub-cut two 17½in squares. Fold your squares into quarters and cut two Flowers template B, taking care to align the corner of the template with the folded corner of your fabric as shown. Keep cut circle and discard outer square.

Step 5: Cut one WOF × 14½in strip of fabric C, sub-cut two 14½in squares. Fold your squares into quarters and cut two Flowers template D, taking care to align the corner of the template with the folded corner of your fabric as shown. Keep cut circle and discard outer square.

Step 6: Cut one WOF × 10in strip each of fabrics D and E and sub-cut four Flowers template H from each fabric.

Flower block

Step 1: Following the Quarter Circle block method described in Chapter 5, use fabric A and fabric D to make four Quarter Circle blocks using Flowers templates G and H. Trim to 9½ × 9½in.

Step 2: Repeat using Flowers templates G and H in fabric A and fabric E to make four Quarter Circle blocks. Trim to 9½ × 9½in.

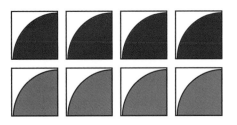

Step 3: Using fabric D Quarter Circle blocks in a Four-Patch arrangement, assemble a Flower block.

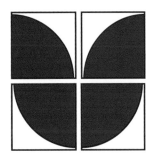
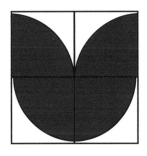

Step 4: Repeat with fabric E Quarter Circle blocks to make a second Flower block.

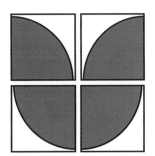
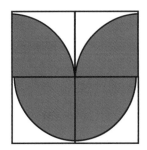

TOP TIP

Don't be tempted to pre-cut your fabric into rings as these are very stretchy and will give unreliable and puckered results.

Inset Circle Block

Step 1: Following the Inset Circles method described in Chapter 5, use 18½in square of fabric A with Flowers template A cut out and circle of fabric B, to insert fabric B circle into fabric A. Finger press and pin at the eighth marks. Press seams outwards before adding the next inset circle.

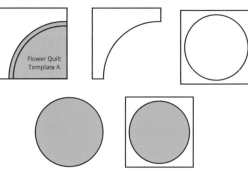

Step 2: Fold block into four and cut out Flowers template C as shown.

Step 3: Insert circle of fabric C into block.

Step 4: Fold block into four and cut out Flowers template E as shown.

Step 4: Insert circle of fabric A into block.

Step 5: Repeat to make two Inset Circle blocks.

ASSEMBLY

Step 1: Join Flower and Inset Circle blocks in a Four-Patch construction as shown, pressing the seams on each row in alternating directions as shown to help nest seams when joining rows together. Press final seam open.

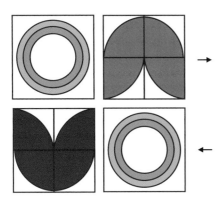

Border
Step 1: Attach 1¼ × 36½in strips to opposite sides of quilt top, pressing seams outward.

Step 2: Attach 1¼ × 38½in strips to opposite sides of quilt top, pressing seams outward.

FINISHING

Step 1: Cut backing yardage to size. If you have directional fabric, you will need more than the given quantity of backing fabric.

Step 2: Baste and quilt as desired.

Step 3: Cut five WOF binding strips. Join and bind using preferred method.

HOW TO QUILT IT

The Flowers sample was quilted using both 40wt and embroidery floss in a combination of machine and hand quilting.

Step 1: With 40wt thread, mark and quilt lines 1in in two directions across fabric A as shown.

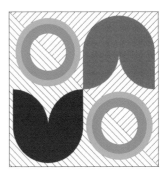

Step 2: In the inset circles, quilt concentric circles ¼in apart.

Step 3: In the flower petals, quilt concentric echoing lines ½in apart as shown. Repeat with the remaining petals.

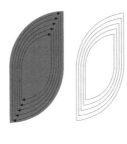

Step 4: Add embroidered stamens using embroidery floss to the flowers.

Step 5: Hand bind with a blind stitch.

STARDUST

The perfect colour companion to Rose Thorns, the small star blocks of Stardust make for a quick and accessible first FPP project. Using one simple star block in two colourways, this cushion adds the perfect colour pop to any room. Add a little hand-quilting to make it extra special and give that luxury factor to your make.

OVERVIEW

You will need
Fabric A: ⅛ yard/metre
Fabric B: ⅛ yard/metre
Fabric C: ⅛ yard/metre
Fabric D: ⅛ yard/metre
Fabric E: ⅜ yard/metre
Binding: ⅛ yard/metre
Backing: ⅝ yards/metres
Lining: ¾ yard/metre
Batting: 47 × 21in
Nine copies of Stardust templates A–F

Fabrics used in sample: Kona Petal (A), Kona Magenta (B), Kona Wisteria (C), Kona Pomegranate (D), Bella Solids White Bleached (E)

Finished measurements
Cushion: 18 × 18in
Blocks: 6 x 6in

Techniques/blocks used
Foundation Paper Piecing (FPP); Nine-Patch construction

PREPARING YOUR TEMPLATES

Step 1: This pattern makes use of one template in two separate colourways. Label the Stardust templates with the correct fabric as shown:

Fabric B: B1, D1, F1 (five blocks)
Fabric C: B1, D1, F1 (four blocks)
Fabric D: A1, C1, E1 (five blocks)
Fabric E: A1, C1, E1 (four blocks)

PIECING

Step 1: Using the Foundation Paper Piecing method described in Chapter 5, piece nine copies of labelled Stardust templates blocks A–F.

Step 2: When you have pieced each of the templates, assemble the blocks by lining up the pattern templates right sides together and matching the points in the following order:

A + B
AB + C
D + E
DE + F
ABC + DEF

Step 3: Gently remove the papers and press the blocks.

TOP TIP

Remove the paper covering the seam allowance after sewing each seam for easier paper removal at the end.

ASSEMBLY

Step 1: Join assembled blocks in a nine-patch construction as shown, pressing the seams on each row in alternating directions as shown to help nest seams when joining rows together. Press final seams open.

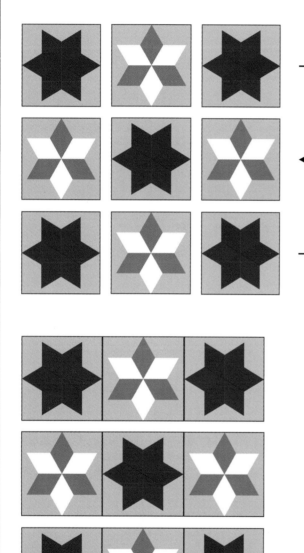

FINISHING

Step 1: Make a quilt sandwich using the pieced cushion front, 21 × 21in batting and lining and quilt as desired.

Step 2: Trim the quilted cushion front as shown to measure 18½ × 18½in, discarding the trimmed sides.

Step 3: Make two back-panel quilt sandwiches using 21 × 13in backing fabric, lining and batting, and quilt as desired.

Step 4: Trim quilted back panels to measure 18½ × 12in and bind one long edge on each panel using your preferred method.

Step 5: With right sides together, fold and sew the front panel and top back panel together along the top edge using a ¼in seam. Sew along the sides of the back panel, back-stitching over the bound edge to make it secure.

Step 6: With right sides together, fold and sew the front panel and bottom back panel together along the bottom edge using a ¼in seam. Seam along the back panel, back-stitching over the bound edge.

Step 7: Turn the cushion right sides out and press the seams carefully to give crisp corners and edges.

HOW TO QUILT IT

The Stardust sample was hand quilted using 12wt thread in a simple echoing design as well as machine quilted with 40wt thread.

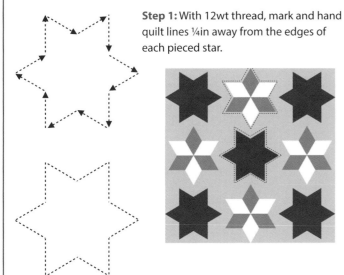

Step 1: With 12wt thread, mark and hand quilt lines ¼in away from the edges of each pieced star.

Step 2: With 40wt thread, mark and machine quilt 1in horizontal lines across both back panel quilt sandwiches.

Step 3: Hand bind with a blind stitch.

HONEYCOMB

The slow stitching pace of English Paper Piecing makes it great for taking on the go or fitting in between other projects when you need a change of pace. Many quilters find they have at least one EPP project on the back burner at any one time. While hand piecing a full-scale quilt can be a bit overwhelming, Honeycomb comes together much more quickly to make a very satisfying finish.

OVERVIEW

You will need
Fabric A: ⅛ yard/metre
Fabric B: ¼ yard/metre
Fabric C: ¼ yard/metre
Fabric D: ⅛ yard/metre
Fabric E (background): ⅜ yard/metre
Binding: ⅛ yard/metre
Backing: ⅝ yard/metres
Lining: ¾ yard/metre
Batting: 51 × 23in
One copy of hexie fabric cutting template
104 copies of hexie paper template (make 10 copies of full-page hexie paper template)

Fabrics used in sample: Kona Sunny (A), Kona Lake (B), Kona Turquoise (C), Kona Riviera (D), Bella Solids White Bleached (E)

Finished measurements
Cushion:19½ × 19½in

Techniques/blocks used
English Paper Piecing (EPP)

CUTTING

Step 1: Using hexie fabric cutting template, cut 12 fabric A.

Step 2: Using hexie fabric cutting template, cut 24 fabric B.

Step 3: Using hexie fabric cutting template, cut 23 fabric C.

Step 4: Using hexie fabric cutting template, cut nine fabric D.

Step 5: Using hexie fabric cutting template, cut 36 fabric E.

BASTING

Step 1: Using preferred basting technique as described in Chapter 5, baste your hexies.

TOP TIP

Take care to ensure your hexies are orientated along the correct sides before starting to sew.

Step 1: Using the method described in Chapter 5, sew three each of sections 1, 2 and 3. Using fabrics A, B, C and D, six of section 4 using fabric E and two of section 5 using fabric E together in the order shown, folding the hexies as needed to ensure you are always sewing along a flat edge.

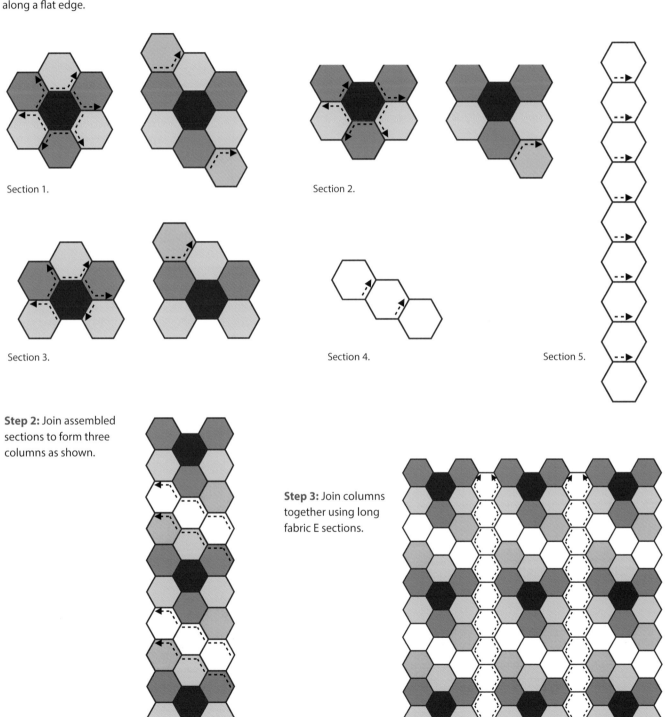

Section 1.

Section 2.

Section 3.

Section 4.

Section 5.

Step 2: Join assembled sections to form three columns as shown.

Step 3: Join columns together using long fabric E sections.

FINISHING

Step 1: Make a quilt sandwich using the pieced cushion front, 23 × 23in batting and lining and quilt as desired.

Step 2: Trim the quilted cushion front as shown to measure 19½ × 19½in, discarding the trimmed sides.

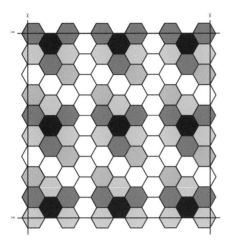

Step 3: Make two back panel quilt sandwiches using 22 × 14in backing fabric, lining and batting and quilt as desired.

Step 4: Trim quilted back panels to measure 19½ × 13in and bind one long edge on each panel using your preferred method.

Step 5: With right sides together, fold and sew the front panel and top back panel together along the top edge using a ¼in seam. Sew along the sides of the back panel, backstitching over the bound edge to make it secure.

Step 6: With right sides together, fold and sew the front panel and bottom back panel together along the bottom edge using a ¼in seam. Seam along the back panel, backstitching over the bound edge.

Step 7: Turn the cushion right sides out and press the seams carefully to give crisp corners and edges.

HOW TO QUILT IT?

The Honeycomb sample was quilted using 40wt thread in a simple diamond design.

Step 1: Mark and sew lines 1⅛in apart using the points and sides of the hexies as a guide as shown.

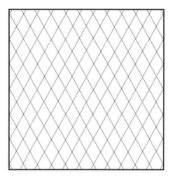

Step 2: With 40wt thread, mark and machine quilt 1in horizontal lines across both back panel quilt sandwiches.

Step 3: Machine bind using a straight stitch.

CHAPTER 8

BLOCK TABLES AND FORMULA

After making a few quilts from patterns, many quilters want to branch out and try their hand at making their own designs to fit their own specific desires, which is where block tables come in. Tweaking and adapting common blocks to fit your needs can be intimidating if you don't know what size fabric to cut for that specific block size.

Block tables are handy reference guides that let you pick the desired finished block size (remember the assembled block will be ½in larger to include a ¼in seam allowance) and quickly see what size of each fabric you will need to cut to produce that size block.

Here you'll find block tables for the most common quilt blocks giving finished sizes from 2in to 12in, as well as the formula used to calculate the tables so that if you want a size not included you can easily work it out for yourself.

Have some fun and play around with mixing and matching different blocks and sizes – get creative!

GENERAL FORMULA

Backing calculation

Yardage formula:

$$\frac{\text{Finished quilt width in} + \text{finished quilt height in}}{36}$$

Metrage formula:

$$\frac{\text{Finished quilt width in} + \text{finished quilt height in}}{39}$$

Yard to metre conversion

Yards to metres conversion formula:
1 yard (36in) = 0.91m

$$\frac{\text{Number of yards}}{1.094} = \text{Number of metres}$$

Metres to yards conversion formula:
1 metre (39.4in) = 1.09 yd

$$\text{Number of metres} \times 1.094 = \text{Number of yards}$$

Binding calculation

Binding length formula:
$(2 \times (\text{finished quilt height in} + \text{finished quilt width in})) + 20$ in

Width of Fabric (WOF) strips calculation:

$$\frac{\text{Binding length in}}{42}$$

Fat Quarter strips calculation:

$$\frac{\text{Binding length in}}{21}$$

BLOCK TABLES

Four-Patch

Formula:
$$\text{All starting squares} = \frac{\text{Finished block size}}{2} + \tfrac{1}{2}\text{in}$$

Finished block size	Unfinished block size	Starting square size
2 × 2in	2½ × 2½in	1½ × 1½in
3 × 3in	3½ × 3½in	2 × 2in
4 × 4in	4½ × 4½in	2½ × 2½in
5 × 5in	5½ × 5½in	3 × 3in
6 × 6in	6½ × 6½in	3½ × 3½in
7 × 7in	7½ × 7½in	4 × 4in
8 × 8in	8½ × 8½in	4½ × 4½in
9 × 9in	9½ × 9½in	5 × 5in
10 × 10in	10½ × 10½in	5½ × 5½in
11 × 11in	11½ × 11½in	6 × 6in
12 × 12in	12½ × 12½in	6½ × 6½in

Nine-Patch

Formula:
$$\text{All starting squares} = \frac{\text{Finished block size}}{3} + \tfrac{1}{2}\text{in}$$

Finished block size	Unfinished block size	Starting square size
3 × 3in	3½ × 3½in	1½ × 1½in
4½ × 4½in	5 × 5in	2 × 2in
6 × 6in	6½ × 6½in	2½ × 2½in
7½ × 7½in	8 × 8in	3 × 3in
9 × 9in	9½ × 9½in	3½ × 3½in
10½ × 10½in	11 × 11in	4 × 4in
12 × 12in	12½ × 12½in	4½ × 4½in

Disappearing Nine-Patch

Formula:
$$\text{All starting squares} = \frac{\text{Finished block size} + 2\text{in}}{3}$$

Finished block size	Unfinished block size	Starting square size
2½ × 2½in	3 × 3in	1½ × 1½in
4 × 4in	4½ × 4½in	2 × 2in
5½ × 5½in	6 × 6in	2½ × 2½in
7 × 7in	7½ × 7½in	3 × 3in
8½ × 8½in	9 × 9in	3½ × 3½in
10 × 10in	10½ × 10½in	4 × 4in
11½ × 11½in	12 × 12in	4½ × 4½in

Half-Square Triangles
Two-at-a-time Half-Square Triangles

Formula:
Both starting squares = Finished block size + 1in

Finished block size	Unfinished block size	Starting square size
2 × 2in	2½ × 2½in	3 × 3in
3 × 3in	3½ × 3½in	4 × 4in
4 × 4in	4½ × 4½in	5 × 5in
5 × 5in	5½ × 5½in	6 × 6in
6 × 6in	6½ × 6½in	7 × 7in
7 × 7in	7½ × 7½in	8 × 8in
8 × 8in	8½ × 8½in	9 × 9in
9 × 9in	9½ × 9½in	10 × 10in
10 × 10in	10½ × 10½in	11 × 11in
11 × 11in	11½ × 11½in	12 × 12in
12 × 12in	12½ × 12½in	13 × 13in

Note: These starting measurements will produce slightly oversized unfinished blocks to allow for accurate trimming. If you prefer not to trim, reduce the starting sizes by ⅛in.

Eight-at-a-time Half-Square Triangles

Formula:
Both starting squares = (2 × Finished block size) +2in

Finished block size	Unfinished block size	Starting square size
2 × 2in	2½ × 2½in	6 × 6in
3 × 3in	3½ × 3½in	8 × 8in
4 × 4in	4½ × 4½in	10 × 10in
5 × 5in	5½ × 5½in	12 × 12in
6 × 6in	6½ × 6½in	14 × 14in
7 × 7in	7½ × 7½in	16 × 16in
8 × 8in	8½ × 8½in	18 × 18in
9 × 9in	9½ × 9½in	20 × 20in
10 × 10in	10½ × 10½in	22 × 22in
11 × 11in	11½ × 11½in	24 × 24in
12 × 12in	12½ × 12½in	26 × 26in

Note: These starting measurements will produce slightly oversized unfinished blocks to allow for accurate trimming. If you prefer not to trim, reduce the starting sizes by ¼in.

Quarter-Square Triangles
Standard

Formula:
All starting squares = Finished block size + 1½in
Four-colour QSTs – you will need one starting square of each colour.
Three-colour QSTs – you will need two starting squares of colour one and one starting square each of colours two and three.
Two-colour QSTs – you will need two starting squares of each colour.

Finished block size	Unfinished block size	Starting square size	Centre point for trimming
2 × 2in	2½ × 2½in	3½ × 3½in	1¼in
3 × 3in	3½ × 3½in	4½ × 4½in	1¾in
4 × 4in	4½ × 4½in	5½ × 5½in	2¼in
5 × 5in	5½ × 5½in	6½ × 6½in	2¾in
6 × 6in	6½ × 6½in	7½ × 7½in	3¼in
7 × 7in	7½ × 7½in	8½ × 8½in	3¾in
8 × 8in	8½ × 8½in	9½ × 9½in	4¼in
9 × 9in	9½ × 9½in	10½ × 10½in	4¾in
10 × 10in	10½ × 10½in	11½ × 11½in	5¼in
11 × 11in	11½ × 11½in	12½ × 12½in	5¾in
12 × 12in	12½ × 12½in	13½ × 13½in	6¼in

Note: These starting measurements will produce slightly oversized unfinished blocks to allow for accurate trimming. If you prefer not to trim, reduce the starting sizes by ⅛in.

Split Quarter-Square Triangles

Formula:
A and B starting squares = Finished block size + 1½in
C starting square = Finished block size + 1in

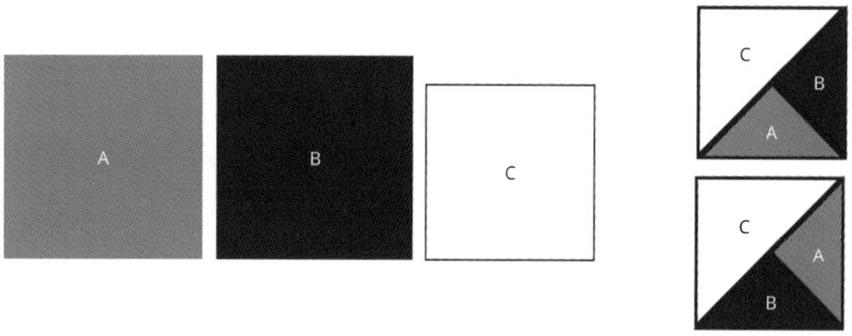

Finished block size	Unfinished block size	Starting squares A and B size	Starting square C size	Centre point for trimming
2 × 2in	2½ × 2½in	3½ × 3½in	3 × 3in	1¼in
3 × 3in	3½ × 3½in	4½ × 4½in	4 × 4in	1¾in
4 × 4in	4½ × 4½in	5½ × 5½in	5 × 5in	2¼in
5 × 5in	5½ × 5½in	6½ × 6½in	6 × 6in	2¾in
6 × 6in	6½ × 6½in	7½ × 7½in	7 × 7in	3¼in
7 × 7in	7½ × 7½in	8½ × 8½in	8 × 8in	3¾in
8 × 8in	8½ × 8½in	9½ × 9½in	9 × 9in	4¼in
9 × 9in	9½ × 9½in	10½ × 10½in	10 × 10in	4¾in
10 × 10in	10½ × 10½in	11½ × 11½in	11 × 11in	5¼in
11 × 11in	11½ × 11½in	12½ × 12½in	12 × 12in	5¾in
12 × 12in	12½ × 12½in	13½ × 13½in	13 × 13in	6¼in

Note: These starting measurements will produce slightly oversized unfinished blocks to allow for accurate trimming. If you prefer not to trim, reduce the starting sizes by ⅛in.

Flying Geese
One-at-a-time Flying Geese

Formula:
A starting rectangle width = Finished block width + ⅝in
A starting rectangle height = Finished block height + ⅝in
B starting squares = Finished block height + ⅝in

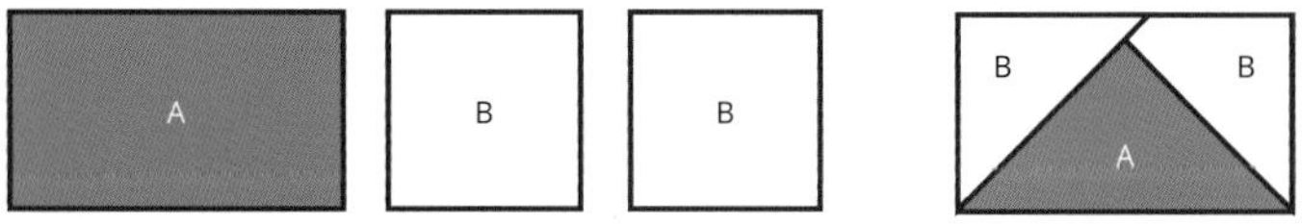

Finished block size	Unfinished block size	Starting rectangle A size	Starting square B size
2 × 4in	2½ × 4½in	3⅛ × 4⅝in	3⅛ × 3⅛in
2½ × 5in	3 × 5½in	3⅝ × 5⅝in	3⅝in × 3⅝in
3 × 6in	3½ × 6½in	4⅛ × 6⅝in	4⅛ × 4⅛in
3½ × 7in	4 × 7½in	4⅝ × 7⅝in	4⅝ × 4⅝in
4 × 8in	4½ × 8½in	5⅛ × 8⅝in	5⅛ × 5⅛in
4½ × 9in	5 × 9½in	5⅝ × 9⅝in	5⅝ × 5⅝in
5 × 10in	5½ × 10½in	6⅛ × 10⅝in	6⅛ × 6⅛in
5½ × 11in	6 × 11½in	6⅝ × 11⅝in	6⅝ × 6⅝in
6 × 12in	6½ × 12½in	7⅛ × 12⅝in	7⅛ × 7⅛in

Note: These starting measurements will produce slightly oversized unfinished blocks to allow for accurate trimming. If you prefer not to trim, reduce the starting sizes by ⅛in.

Four-at-a-time Flying Geese

Formula:
A starting square = Finished block width + 1½in
B starting squares = Finished block height + 1in

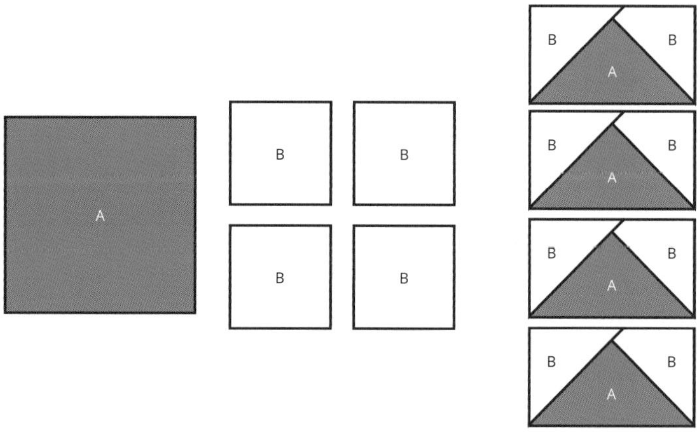

Finished block size	Unfinished block size	Starting square A size	Starting square B size
2 × 4in	2½ × 4½in	5½ × 5½in	3 × 3in
2½ × 5in	3 × 4½in	6½ × 6½in	3½ × 3½in
3 × 6in	3½ × 6½in	7½ × 7½in	4 × 4in
3½ × 7in	4 × 7½in	8½ × 8½in	4½ × 4½in
4 × 8in	4½ × 8½in	9½ × 9½in	5 × 5in
4½ × 9in	5 × 9½in	10½ × 10½in	5½ × 5½in
5 × 10in	5½ × 10½in	11½ × 11½in	6 × 6in
5½ × 11in	6 × 11½in	12½ × 12½in	6½ × 6½in
6 × 12in	6½ × 12½in	13½ × 13½in	7 × 7in

Note: These starting measurements will produce slightly oversized unfinished blocks to allow for accurate trimming. If you prefer not to trim, reduce the starting sizes by ⅛in.

Half-Rectangle Triangles

Formula:
Both starting rectangles width = Finished block width + 1in
Both starting rectangles height = Finished block height + 2in

Finished block size	Unfinished block size	Starting rectangle size
2 × 4in	2½ × 4½in	3 × 6in
2½ × 5in	3 × 4½in	3½ × 7in
3 × 6in	3½ × 6½in	4 × 8in
3½ × 7in	4 × 7½in	4½ × 9in
4 × 8in	4½ × 8½in	5 × 10in
4½ × 9in	5 × 9½in	5½ × 11in
5 × 10in	5½ × 10½in	6 × 12in
5½ × 11in	6 × 11½in	6½ × 13in
6 × 12in	6½ × 12½in	7 × 14in

Note: These starting measurements will produce slightly oversized unfinished blocks to allow for accurate trimming.

Single Square-in-a-Square
Stitch and flip method

Formula:
A starting square = Finished block size + ½in

$$\text{B starting squares} = \frac{\text{Finished block size}}{2} + \tfrac{1}{2}\text{in}$$

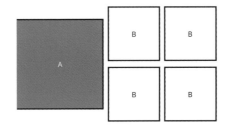

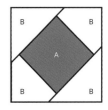

Finished block size	Unfinished block size	Starting square A size	Starting squares B size
2 × 2in	2½ × 2½in	2½ × 2½in	1½ × 1½in
3 × 3in	3½ × 3½in	3½ × 3½in	2 × 2in
4 × 4in	4½ × 4½in	4½ × 4½in	2½ × 2½in
5 × 5in	5½ × 5½in	5½ × 5½in	3 × 3in
6 × 6in	6½ × 6½in	6½ × 6½in	3½ × 3½in
7 × 7in	7½ × 7½in	7½ × 7½in	4 × 4in
8 × 8in	8½ × 8½in	8½ × 8½in	4½ × 4½in
9 × 9in	9½ × 9½in	9½ × 9½in	5 × 5in
10 × 10in	10½ × 10½in	10½ × 10½in	5½ × 5½in
11 × 11in	11½ × 11½in	11½ × 11½in	6 × 6in
12 × 12in	12½ × 12½in	12½ × 12½in	6½ × 6½in

Triangles method

Formula:

A starting square = $\dfrac{\text{Finished block size}}{1\frac{7}{16}}$ + ½in (round up to the nearest ⅛in)

Note:

$1\frac{7}{16} = 1.44$

B starting squares to be cut diagonally = $\dfrac{\text{Finished block size}}{2}$ + ⅞in

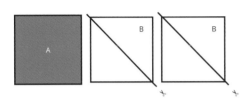 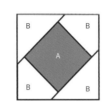

Finished block size	Unfinished block size	Starting square A size	Starting squares B size
2 × 2in	2½ × 2½in	2 × 2in	1⅞ × 1⅞in
3 × 3in	3½ × 3½in	2⅝ × 2⅝in	2⅜ × 2⅜in
4 × 4in	4½ × 4½in	3⅜ × 3⅜in	2⅞ × 2⅞in
5 × 5in	5½ × 5½in	4 × 4in	3⅜ × 3⅜in
6 × 6in	6½ × 6½in	4¾ × 4¾in	3⅞ × 3⅞in
7 × 7in	7½ × 7½in	5⅜ × 5⅜in	4⅜ × 4⅜in
8 × 8in	8½ × 8½in	6⅛ × 6⅛in	4⅞ × 4⅞in
9 × 9in	9½ × 9½in	6¾ × 6¾in	5⅜ × 5⅜in
10 × 10in	10½ × 10½in	7½ × 7½in	5⅞ × 5⅞in
11 × 11in	11½ × 11½in	8¼ × 8¼in	6⅜ × 6⅜in
12 × 12in	12½ × 12½in	8⅞ × 8⅞in	6⅞ × 6⅞in

Double Square-in-a-Square

Formula:

A starting square = $\dfrac{\text{Finished block size}}{2}$ + ½in

B starting squares to be cut diagonally = $\dfrac{\text{Finished block size} \div 2}{1\frac{7}{16}}$ + ⅞in (round up to the nearest ¼in)

Note:

$1\frac{7}{16} = 1.44$

C starting squares to be cut diagonally = $\dfrac{\text{Finished block size}}{2}$ + ⅞in

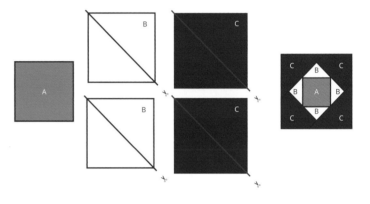

Finished block size	Unfinished block size	Starting square A size	Starting squares B size	Starting squares C size
2 × 2in	2½ × 2½in	1½ × 1½in	1¾ × 1¾in	1⅞ × 1⅞in
3 × 3in	3½ × 3½in	2 × 2in	2 × 2in	2⅜ × 2⅜in
4 × 4in	4½ × 4½in	2½ × 2½in	2½ × 2½in	2⅞ × 2⅞in
5 × 5in	5½ × 5½in	3 × 3in	2¾ × 2¾in	3⅜ × 3⅜in
6 × 6in	6½ × 6½in	3½ × 3½in	3 × 3in	3⅞ × 3⅞in
7 × 7in	7½ × 7½in	4 × 4in	3½ × 3½in	4⅜ × 4⅜in
8 × 8in	8½ × 8½in	4½ × 4½in	3¾ × 3¾in	4⅞ × 4⅞in
9 × 9in	9½ × 9½in	5 × 5in	4 × 4in	5⅜ × 5⅜in
10 × 10in	10½ × 10½in	5½ × 5½in	4½ × 4½in	5⅞ × 5⅞in
11 × 11in	11½ × 11½in	6 × 6in	4¾ × 4¾in	6⅜ × 6⅜in
12 × 12in	12½ × 12½in	6½ × 6½in	5¼ × 5¼in	6⅞ × 6⅞in

Note: Starting squares B measurements will produce slightly oversized unfinished blocks to allow for accurate trimming before adding starting squares C.

Inset Circles

Formula:
A starting circle = Finished circle diameter + ½in
B starting circle = Finished circle diameter − ½in

 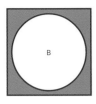 

Finished circle diameter	Starting circle A diameter	Starting circle B diameter
6in	6½in	5½in
7in	7½in	6½in
8in	8½in	7½in
9in	9½in	8½in
10in	10½in	9½in
11in	11½in	10½in
12in	12½in	11½in

TEMPLATES

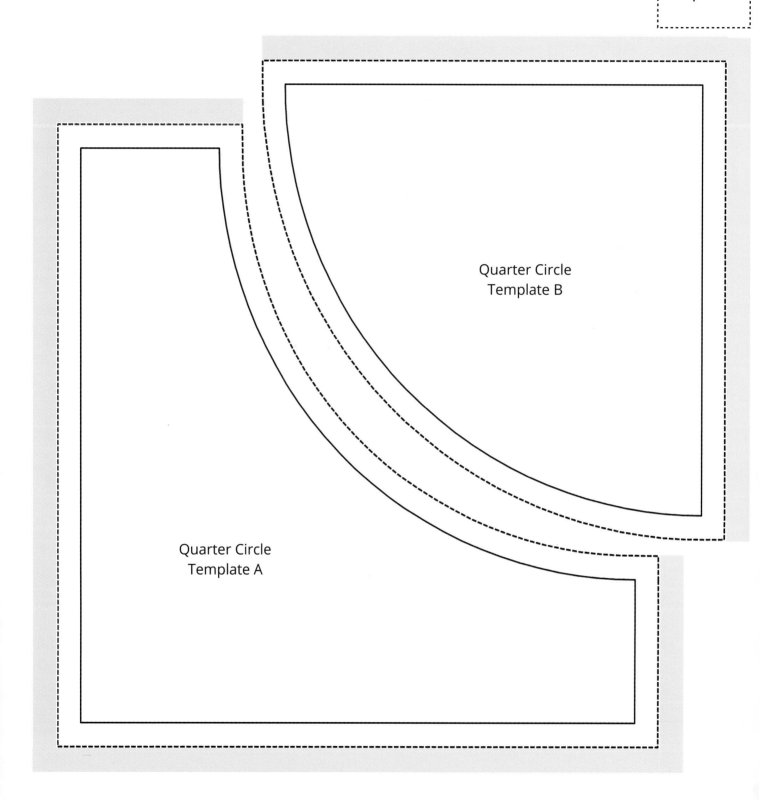

1" test square

Quarter Circle
Template B

Quarter Circle
Template A

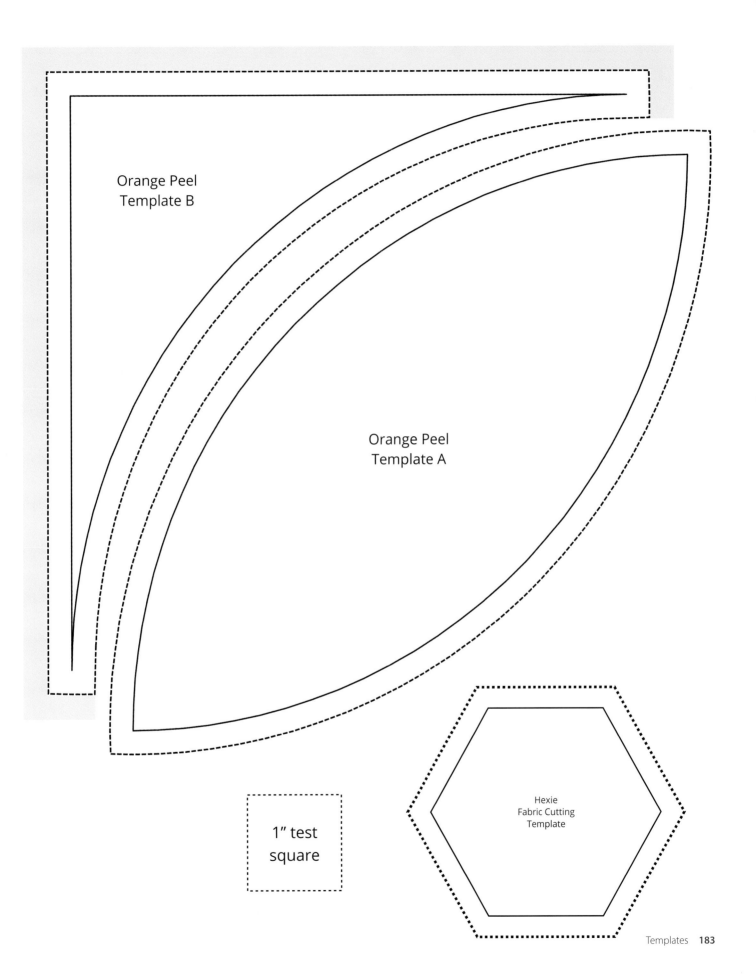

Orange Peel
Template B

Orange Peel
Template A

1" test
square

Hexie
Fabric Cutting
Template

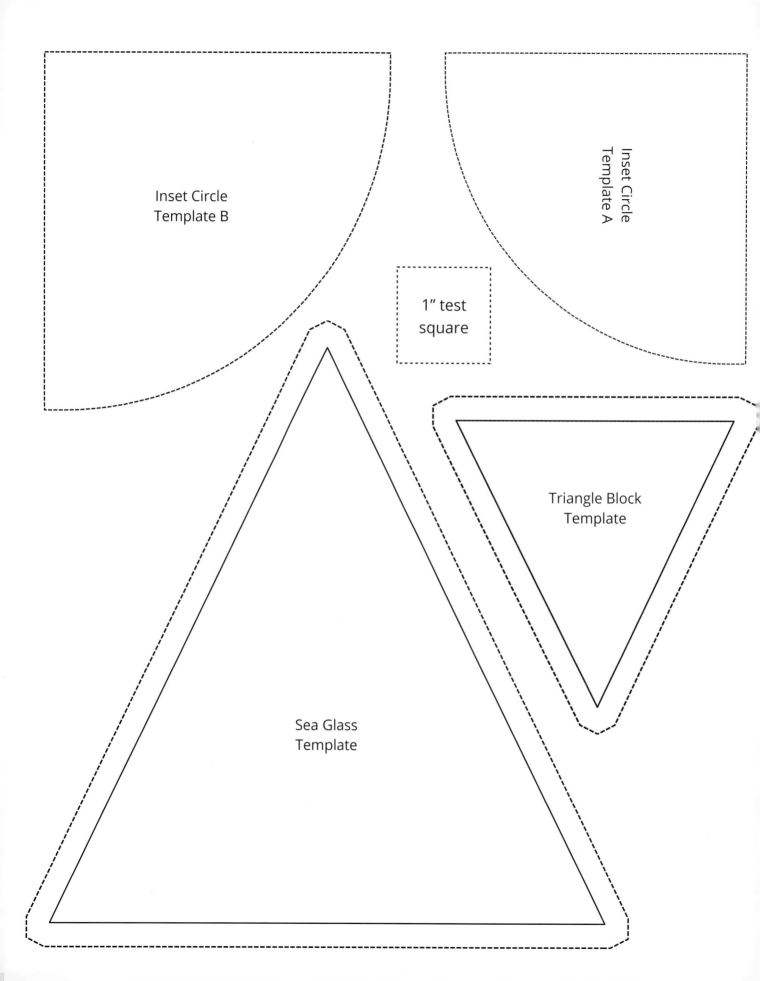

Inset Circle
Template B

Inset Circle
Template A

1" test
square

Triangle Block
Template

Sea Glass
Template

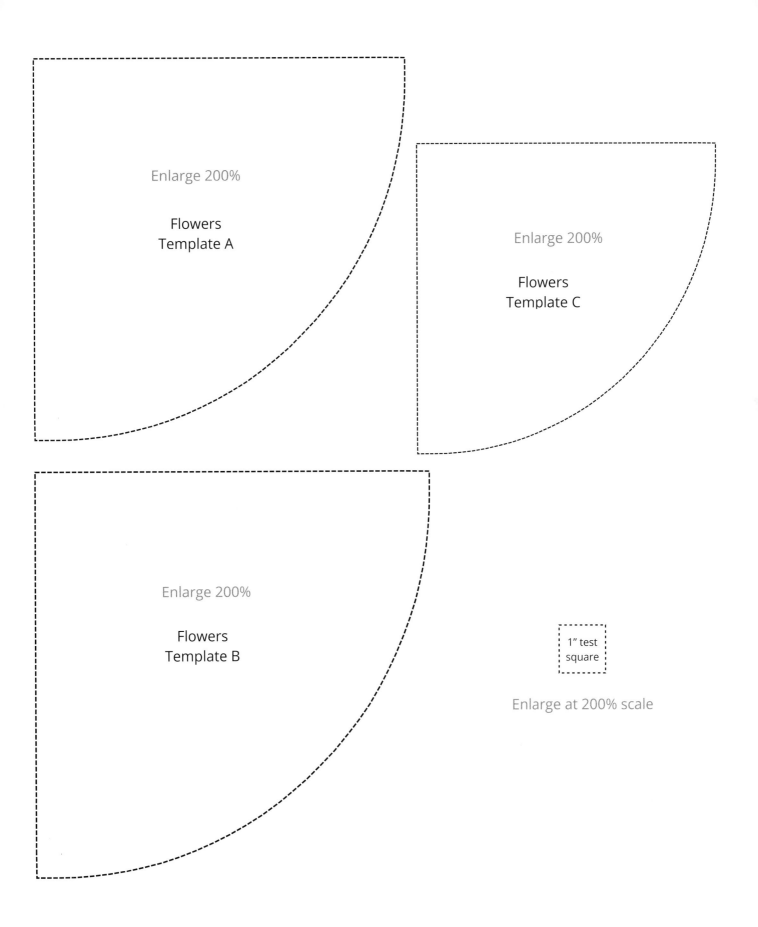

Enlarge 200%

Flowers
Template A

Enlarge 200%

Flowers
Template C

Enlarge 200%

Flowers
Template B

1" test
square

Enlarge at 200% scale

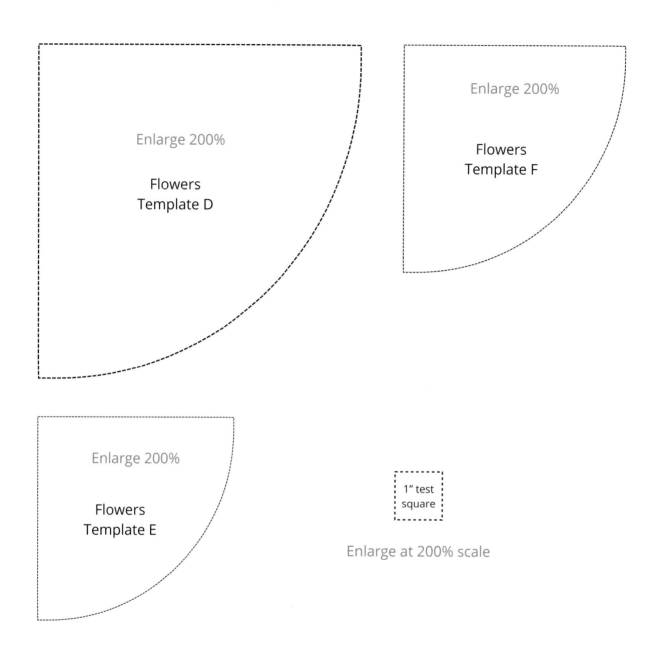

Enlarge 200%

Flowers
Template D

Enlarge 200%

Flowers
Template F

Enlarge 200%

Flowers
Template E

1" test
square

Enlarge at 200% scale

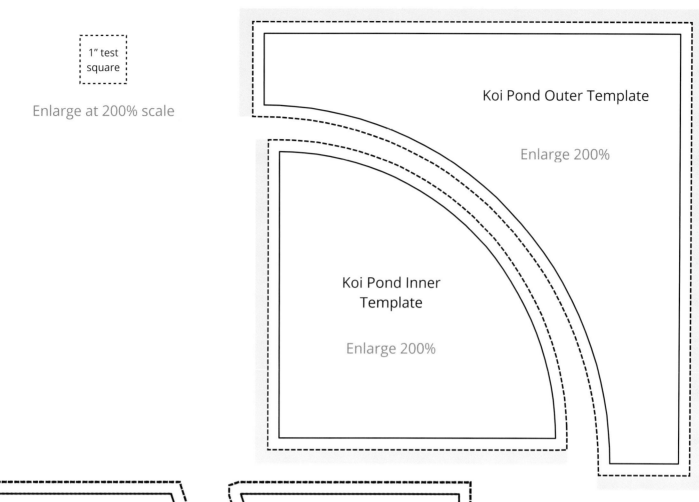

1" test
square

Enlarge at 200% scale

Koi Pond Outer Template

Enlarge 200%

Koi Pond Inner
Template

Enlarge 200%

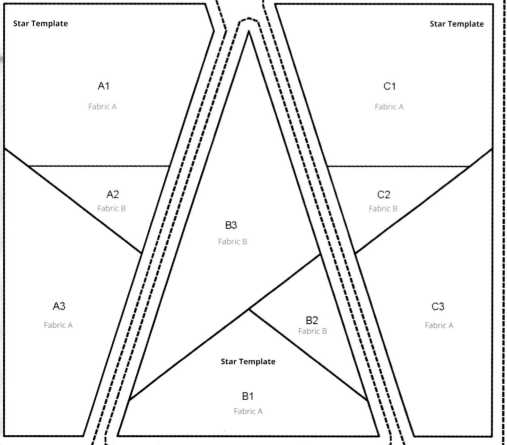

Star Template

A1

Fabric A

A2

Fabric B

A3

Fabric A

B3

Fabric B

B2

Fabric B

Star Template

B1

Fabric A

Star Template

C1

Fabric A

C2

Fabric B

C3

Fabric A

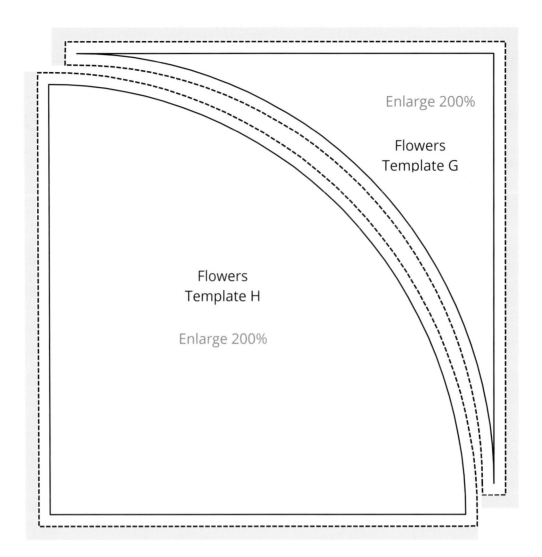

Enlarge 200%

Flowers
Template G

Flowers
Template H

Enlarge 200%

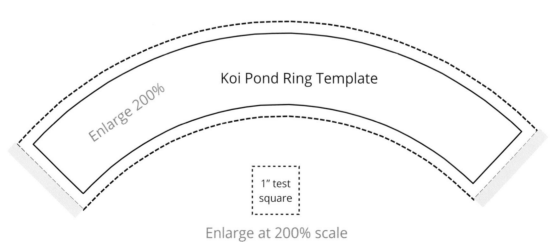

Koi Pond Ring Template

Enlarge 200%

1" test
square

Enlarge at 200% scale

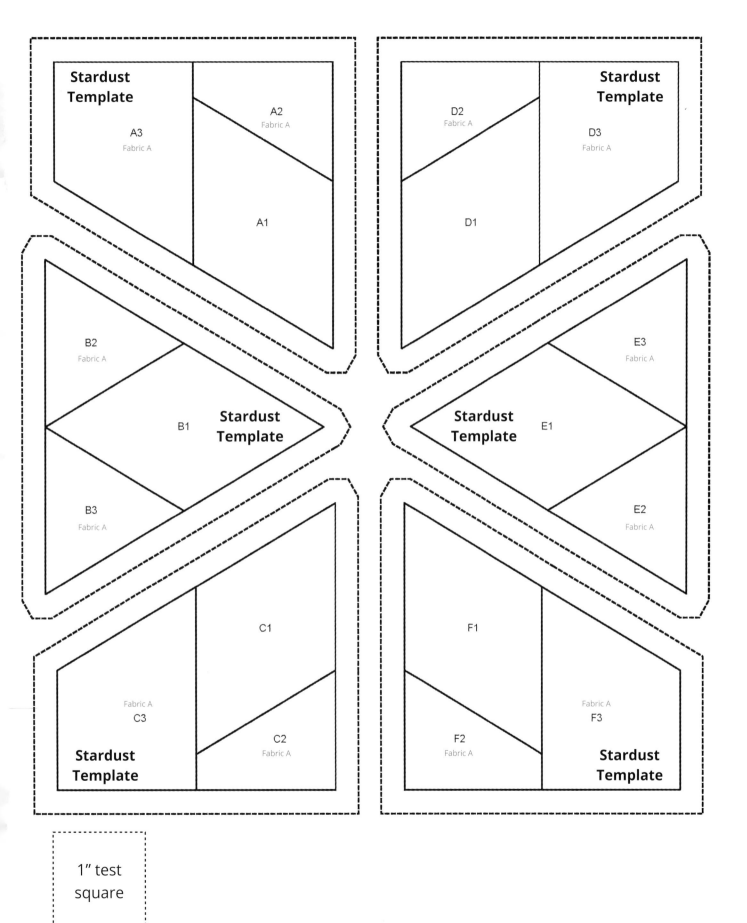

Stardust Template

A3
Fabric A

A2
Fabric A

A1

Stardust Template

D2
Fabric A

D3
Fabric A

D1

B2
Fabric A

B1

Stardust Template

B3
Fabric A

Stardust Template

E1

E3
Fabric A

E2
Fabric A

C1

Fabric A
C3

C2
Fabric A

Stardust Template

F1

F2
Fabric A

Fabric A
F3

Stardust Template

1" test square

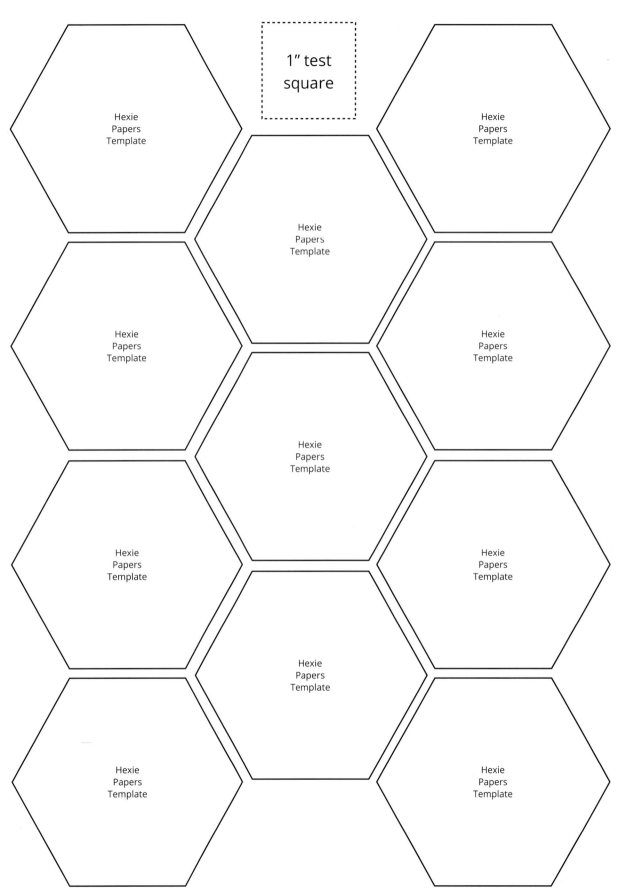

1" test
square

Hexie
Papers
Template

Hexie
Papers
Template

Hexie
Papers
Template

Hexie
Papers
Template

Hexie
Papers
Template

Hexie
Papers
Template

Hexie
Papers
Template

Hexie
Papers
Template

Hexie
Papers
Template

Hexie
Papers
Template

Hexie
Papers
Template

INDEX

First published in 2024 by
The Crowood Press Ltd
Ramsbury, Marlborough
Wiltshire SN8 2HR

enquiries@crowood.com
www.crowood.com

British Library Cataloguing-in-Publication Data
A catalogue record for this book is available from the British Library.

ISBN 978 0 7198 4408 9

Cover design by Sergey Tsvetkov
Photos: Sadie Windscheffel-Clarke, Big Fish Photography
Technical editing: Elisabeth Myrick, Elisabeth Quilt Co.

Graphic design and typesetting by Peggy & Co. Design
Printed and bound in India by Nutech Print Services - India

Acknowledgements

This book is dedicated to my wife Ashley, without whose unending support this book would not have been possible. There aren't enough words in the world to express my gratitude for your love and encouragement through all the highs and lows of such a huge undertaking. I love you more than I can ever say.

Thanks also to my feline Quality Inspectors, Lyra and Aurora, for their commitment to ensuring every quilt I make has been properly imbued with fur and for always sitting on the block I need to sew.

Huge thanks to Sadie Windscheffel-Clarke for throwing yourself into the weird and wonderful world of quilt photography with so much enthusiasm, you made my quilts look truly stunning. Thank you also to Elisabeth Myrick for your excellent technical editing skills.

Finally, thank you to the quilting community for making me feel welcome ever since I first dipped my toes into this wonderful fabric world, and especially the Cambridgeshire MQG for riding the roller coaster of this book alongside me and always cheering me on.